Mastering Reading
Skills for Success
Book 1
Food Service

Robert Ventre Associates, Inc.
Ellen Kisslinger

Delmar Occupational Learning System®

NOTICE TO THE READER

Photo location courtesy of Capital District Educational Opportunity Center, 145 Congress Street, Troy, New York 12180, phone number (518) 273-1900, a Division of Hudson Valley Community College, part of the State University of New York.

Photo by Joseph Schuyler Photography.

Delmar Staff:
Executive Editor: David C. Gordon
Project Editor: Judith Boyd Nelson
Production Coordinator: Teresa Luterbach
Art Coordinator: Michael J. Nelson

For information, address Delmar Publishers Inc.
2 Computer Drive, West, Box 15-015,
Albany, NY 12212-9985

ISBN 0-8273-4467-8

CONTENTS

PHOTO ACKNOWLEDGMENTS

pp. 2, 50: From Robert Ventre Associates, *Learning About Health Care,* copyright 1990 by Delmar Publishers Inc.

p. 80: From Simmers, *Diversified Health Occupations,* 2nd edition, copyright 1988 by Delmar Publishers Inc.

pp. 32, 117: From Wolfe, *Cooking for the Professional Chef,* copyright 1982 by Delmar Publishers Inc.

TO THE LEARNER

Welcome to *Mastering Reading: Skills for Success, Book 1/Food Service*. All the books in the Food-Service series are written with you, the adult learner, in mind. As you know, being able to read well is very important in the world of today. With good reading skills, you have a much better chance of getting the kind of job you want. Good reading skills also let you move ahead in the job you have. You can learn more about the world you live in.

The book you are about to use will improve your reading skills as you learn about food and self-care. As you read, you will learn some very useful things about food and about taking care of yourself.

Book 1 is made up of 20 lessons. You can look at the **Table of Contents** to see what they are about. Each lesson begins with some questions on the first page. There are no right or wrong answers to these questions. Examples of questions are, "What do you do to get ready to cook?" and "Why is it important to keep the kitchen clean?" These questions let you look at some things that you have already learned in your life. That way, the lesson will make more sense to you. Some of you reading this book will be in a class with other students. If so, your instructor will probably have you talk about these questions as a class. If you are working alone with a tutor, you can discuss your ideas with the tutor.

Each lesson has two pages of reading. Most of the readings are about food. Other readings are about taking care of yourself and getting along in the world. As you read, you will notice that some words are in **boldface**. These bold-faced words are explained in the **Glossary** in the back of the book. The Glossary tells you what each bold-faced word means. After you read the meaning, you will find one or two sentences using that word.

After each reading, you will see exercises. Each lesson has about three pages of exercises. These exercises ask questions that are based on the reading or on your own experience in life. There are two kinds of exercises in each lesson:

- a Review exercise

- two or more Practice exercises

Answers for all the Review and Practice exercises are in the back of the book in the **Answer Key**. You can find the Answer Key just before the Glossary. The Answer Key lets you check your answers and correct them if you need to.

The Review questions have three possible answers to choose from. To find the right answers, you may want to go back and do the reading again. You will probably discuss your answers with people in your class and with your teacher. The first Review question in each lesson is answered for you.

There are many different kinds of Practice exercises. Some exercise questions have just one right answer. Others have more than one answer. These types of Practice exercises will have the words: "More than one answer is possible. Check with your instructor or tutor." With such exercises, each learner might have a different answer. But all those answers would be correct. For example, the question "What did you have for breakfast?" would have many answers. Each answer would be correct for the person giving it.

When you have read *Mastering Reading: Skills for Success, Book 1/Food Service*, you may wish to read *Mastering Reading: Skills for Success, Book 2/Food Service*. This is the next book in the *Mastering Reading: Skills for Success, Food Service* series. *Book 2* also is about food and self-care. But it tells you more about these things.

Book 2 is followed by *Mastering Reading: Learning about Food Service, Book 3* and *Mastering Reading: Learning about Food Service, Book 4*. These books deal more directly with cooking and the field of Food Service. If you think that you may want a career in Food Service, these books will be useful to you. They tell you about some of things you do in the Food-Service field.

Some adult learners reading these books will wish to get a job in Food Service. Other learners will want to read the books to learn how to read better and know more about food. Whatever reason you have, we hope that you are able to enjoy this book and to learn from it. Good Luck!

UNIT 1

Keep It Balanced

This unit is about:

- different types of food

- choosing healthful food

Think About

What did you eat yesterday? Make a list of these foods
  on a piece of paper.
What do you think the title of this unit means?

Keep It Balanced

What did you eat for breakfast? What do you like to eat for a snack? What does the word *diet* mean to you? For some people, it means losing weight. But *diet* has another meaning. It also means all of the food that you usually eat. Newborn babies, for example, have a diet of milk or formula. An adult usually has a diet of many different kinds of food. Each day we have to decide what to eat. What we eat helps **determine**—or decide—how we feel.

The best kind of diet is a **balanced** diet. It helps us stay healthy. A balanced diet includes foods from four main groups. These four groups are: (1) fruits and vegetables, (2) dairy foods, (3) breads and cereals, and (4) meats, beans, and nuts. We need food from these four groups every day.

Knowing the four food groups helps us decide what to eat. Look at the chart below. It shows what an adult needs every day from each food group. The first **column** shows the food groups. The second column shows the number of **servings** adults need to give themselves every day. The third column shows the size of one serving. For example, each day an adult needs at least two servings from the dairy group. A cup of milk is one serving for an adult. Of course, how much we need of each food group depends on how old we are. Babies, children, and adults need different amounts.

Food group	Servings per day for adults	Serving size
Fruits and vegetables	4 or more	1 apple 1 potato $1/2$ cup cooked vegetables $1/2$ cup fruit juice
Dairy foods	2 or more	1 cup milk a one-inch cube hard cheese 1 cup yogurt 3 scoops ice cream
Breads and cereals	4 or more	1 slice bread 5 saltine crackers 1 cup dry cereal half a hamburger bun $1/2$ cup noodles
Meats, nuts, beans, and eggs	2 or more	1 cup beans 1 piece fish 1 hamburger 2 eggs 4 tablespoons peanut butter

To have a balanced diet we need to eat some of each group every day. A balanced diet can help make us strong and healthy. It can give us energy to do what we want to do.

REVIEW

Choose the best answer. Circle it. Go back to the reading to check your answers. The first one is done for you.

1. Which of these statements is true?
    a. All people and animals have the same diet.
    b. Some people do not have a diet.
    c. Your diet is the food you eat.

2. A balanced diet _____.
    a. has different kinds of food
    b. is not good for you
    c. has food from only one food group

3. How many servings of dairy foods does an adult need each day?
    a. two or more
    b. three
    c. four or more

4. How large is one serving of juice in the chart?
    a. 1/2 cup
    b. 1 cup
    c. 1 1/2 cups

5. Which of these foods is in the "meats" food group?
    a. cereal
    b. eggs
    c. yogurt

6. Another title for this reading could be _____.
    a. Eat Meat
    b. How To Lose Weight
    c. A Balanced Diet

PRACTICE

A. Where do these foods belong? Each of the foods below goes in one food group. Put each of these foods in the right food group. The first one is done for you.

apples   corn flakes   fish
milk   peanuts   potatoes

Fruits and Vegetables	Dairy Foods	Breads and Cereals	Meats
	milk		

B. Which food is from a different food group? Each line names four foods. Three foods are from the same food group. One food is from a different food group. Underline the food from a different group. The first one is done for you.

1. chicken   <u>cheese</u>   pork chops   fish

2. bananas   carrots   lemons   yogurt

3. milk   yogurt   cereal   ice cream

4. steak   bread   rolls   crackers

5. grapes   nuts   tomatoes   oranges

6. tomatoes   yogurt   cheese   milk

C. What did you eat yesterday? Look at the list of foods you ate yesterday. Then, answer the questions.

1. Did you have food from all four food groups?

_____

2. If not, which food group is missing from your list?

_____

D. Keep a record of what you eat. List the foods that you eat on this chart. Each time you eat something, write the name of the food in its food group. For example, on Day 1 you have some orange juice and toast for breakfast. Write *orange juice* in the fruits and vegetables group. Write *toast* in the breads and cereals group. Keep a record for two days. Ask your family to do it too. Then, talk about how you can improve your diets.

Food Group	Day 1	Day 2
Fruits and Vegetables	orange juice	
Dairy Foods		
Breads and Cereals	toast	
Meats		

UNIT 2

Good Eating Habits

Think About

When do you eat? Do you like to snack?
Where do you usually eat your meals?
Do you enjoy mealtime? If so, what do you enjoy about it?

Good Eating Habits

When do you eat? Where do you eat? What do you usually do while you are eating? Eating a balanced diet is important. Good eating **habits** are also important. Here are a few suggestions for developing good eating habits so that you can plan your meals in advance.

Eat at regular times. Some people like to eat several small meals. Some people like to eat two or three larger meals. Pay attention to your own needs. However often you eat, try to eat at about the same times each day.

Avoid eating between meals. If you do snack, remember the four food groups. Try choosing cheese and crackers or a banana instead of potato chips. If you eat a candy bar for a snack one day, eat fruit for your snack the next day.

Think about what you eat. At the end of the day, you might want to think about what you ate. Think about the four food groups. Did you forget to eat enough from one group? Try to eat more from that group the next day.

Eat with the weather in mind. Is it warm? Is it cold? In warm weather, you may feel better if you eat lighter foods. Salads are good to eat then. You also need lots of water. Drink at least eight glasses of water every day. In cold weather, most people need heavier foods. Soups and stews help us stay warm. And you still need to drink plenty of water.

Take time to enjoy your meals. Don't eat and work at the same time. Try not to watch TV while you are eating. Sit down at the table. Relax and enjoy your meals with family or friends.

Get in the habit of good eating. Pay attention to what you eat. Think about a balanced diet. You will have more energy, and your mind and body will feel better, too.

REVIEW

Choose the best answer. Circle it. Go back to the reading to check your answers. The first one is done for you.

1. Eating regularly means eating _____.
   a. large meals
   b. small meals
   (c.) at the same time each day

2. Snacks should _____.
   a. always be cheese and crackers
   b. be as balanced as possible
   c. never be candy bars

3. If we think about what we eat, _____.
   a. it is easier to remember to eat right
   b. we can eat more
   c. it is easier to eat only salads

4. In warm weather, many people like to eat _____.
   a. hot soup
   b. lighter foods
   c. stew

5. Water is important in _____.
   a. hot weather
   b. cold weather
   c. both hot and cold weather

6. A good way to enjoy meals is to eat _____.
   a. with friends
   b. while we work
   c. alone in front of the TV

PRACTICE

A. Think about your eating habits. Then, answer the questions below. Put a check mark in the correct column.

	Often	Some-times	Never
1. Do you eat at regular times?			
2. Do you snack?			
3. Do you eat sweet snacks?			
4. Does the weather affect what you eat?			
5. Do you drink lots of water every day?			
6. Do you eat balanced meals?			
7. Do you watch TV during mealtimes?			
8. Do you eat while you work?			
9. Do you sit down at the table to eat?			
10. Do you eat with your family?			

B. What do you suggest? Each of these people needs to develop better eating habits. Read the situation. Then, suggest something that will help each person eat better.

1. A friend's son loves to snack. He eats potato chips and cookies as he watches TV after school. Then, he is not hungry at dinner.

   <u>Your friend should make sure fruits and</u>

   <u>vegetables are around to snack on and hide</u>

   <u>the chips and cookies.</u>

2. Your boss always eats a donut in the car on her way to work. Later, she complains that her stomach hurts her.

   _____

   _____

   _____

3. In the summer Carlos works outside all day. He drinks lots of coffee for breakfast and lunch. He still feels very thirsty.

   _____

   _____

   _____

4. Will is very busy. Sometimes he eats just one meal a day. When he eats, he usually has a hamburger and fries.

   _____

   _____

   _____

UNIT 3

Get Out That List!

This unit is about:

- food shopping habits

Think About

When do you shop?
How do you decide what to buy?
What packaged foods do you regularly buy? Make a list.

Get Out That List!

It is time to go grocery shopping. You know about the four basic food groups. You know how important these four groups are in deciding what to buy at the grocery store. What is a good way to choose what to buy?

Always plan ahead. Plan your main meals for the week. Make a list of things you need. Keep the list on the refrigerator. Write down what you need as you think of it. Check the list before you go shopping. Have you included enough from each food group? At the store, stick to your list!

Find ways to save. The weekly food ads in the newspaper tell you about **specials**—foods with special low prices. **Coupons** also come in the mail. You can use them to save money on **products** you usually buy.

apples
orange juice
2 lbs. hamburger
chicken legs
sour cream
1 gallon milk
cheese
bread
eggs
crackers
tomato soup

SAVE 25¢ With This Coupon
Orange Juice
12 Oz. Can Frozen

FRESH SPECIALS
Bring home fresh and delicious dairy foods for your family.

Chicken Legs 79¢ lb.
3 lbs. or more......

Chicken Leg Quarters
3 lbs or more.....59¢ lb.

Boneless Breasts...2.99 lb.
Skinless

Don't shop on an empty stomach. If you are hungry, everything looks good. It becomes easy to buy on **impulse**, to get whatever you feel like at the time. Advertisers try to get us to buy treats. It is easy to buy treats such as cookies, instead of food that is good for us. If you have to shop before a meal, eat an apple first.

Check what is in your cart. Did you stick to your list? Did you pick up something just because you were hungry or because you liked the package? Put it back! A simple food such as macaroni and cheese can cost more in a fancy box. Also, some packaged foods are better for you than others. Read the **labels** on the front and back of the package carefully.

You want to get as much healthful food as possible for your dollar. This is true whether you are paying with cash or with food stamps. Going grocery shopping is easier if you are organized. Decide what you need before you go. Follow your list. And check your cart before you go to the checkout.

REVIEW

Choose the best answer. Circle it. Go back to the reading to check your answers. The first one is done for you.

1. Before you go shopping, _____.
   a. do not eat
   (b.) make a list
   c. check your cart

2. A list helps you to _____.
   a. buy foods that look good
   b. buy extra food
   c. buy only what you need

3. It is better to go food shopping _____.
   a. right before dinner
   b. after lunch
   c. when you are hungry

4. If you buy on impulse, you _____.
   a. do not follow a list
   b. follow your list
   c. make a list

5. Food in a fancy box _____.
   a. is always better
   b. usually tastes a lot better
   c. can cost a lot more

6. Another title for this reading could be _____.
   a. Reading Newspapers
   b. Shopping Suggestions
   c. Grocery Carts

PRACTICE

A. Choose a word. Complete each sentence with a word or phrase from the reading. Write the answer in the space. The first one is done for you.

cookies   coupons   food ads
macaroni & cheese   refrigerator

1. It is a good idea to check the __**food ads**__ before you shop.

2. Cutting out _____ can help you save money.

3. A good place to keep a list is on the _____.

4. _____ are a kind of treat.

5. An example of a packaged food is _____.

B. Make a shopping list. Think about the food you use in a week. Write your shopping list on the lines below. One idea is given for you.

___a dozen eggs_____

_____

_____

_____

_____

C. Think about your shopping habits. Answer the questions below. Put a check mark in the correct column.

	Often	Some-times	Never
1. Do you make a shopping list?			
2. If you make a list, do you stick to it?			
3. Do you check the newspaper for specials?			
4. Do you try to use coupons?			
5. Do you go shopping on an empty stomach?			
6. Do you buy something because you like the box?			
7. Do you read labels?			
8. Do you check your cart before you go to the checkout?			

D. What do you suggest? A friend is having trouble grocery shopping. He spends a lot of money at the store, but he does not get the things he really needs. What should he do? One suggestion is given. Add some more!

<u>use coupons</u>

_____

_____

UNIT 4

What's in It?

This unit is about:

- reading food labels

- understanding the order of ingredients

Think About

Do you read labels on foods?
What do you look for on the labels?
What would make you decide *not* to buy something?

19

What's in It?

You are at the grocery store. You need some peanut butter. How do you decide which **brand** to buy? One way is to read the labels. A skilled shopper knows how to read labels. Reading carefully helps us spend our food money or food stamps wisely.

Look at the order of the **ingredients** on the label. The law **requires** that the ingredients be listed from most to least. For example, if there is more sugar than salt, sugar must be listed before salt.

You find the **aisle** where the peanut butter is. You notice two brands of peanut butter. You pick up the peanut butter on the left. The label says:

MUNCHY PEANUT BUTTER

ingredients: ground peanuts and salt

Now, you look at the jar on the right. The label says:

YUMMY PEANUT BUTTER

ingredients: ground peanuts, corn syrup, vegetable oil, sugar, and salt

---

Which jar is better? Think back to the four basic food groups. If you are buying the peanut butter as part of the meats group, you want to get the most peanuts for your money. The jar on the left is better. You will get more peanuts in each serving.

Look at some of the products in the supermarket. Read the labels carefully. For example, the label on one box of cereal says the cereal has real honey. You read the label. You notice that honey is the last ingredient listed. This means there is very little honey in it.

```
HONEY BREAKFAST CEREAL

ingredients:  wheat, sugar, wheat
         bran, salt, honey
```

Another example is bread. Some bread labels say the bread contains real butter. Look at the label carefully. The butter is listed after the salt. Most bread has only a little salt in it. You know there cannot be much butter in the bread.

```
GREAT BREAD:  Made with
      Real Butter

ingredients:  enriched wheat
   flour, water, whole wheat
   flour, sugar, vegetable oil,
      yeast, salt, butter
```

Being a good shopper means being a label **detective**. A label detective reads labels carefully and always remembers the four basic food groups. When you shop, ask yourself some questions: What are the ingredients? In what order are they listed? Is this a good food for a balanced diet?

REVIEW

Choose the best answer. Circle it. Go back to the reading to check your answers. The first one is done for you.

1. Reading _____ helps us decide which brand to buy.
   a. sizes
   b. labels
   c. flavors

2. Ingredients are listed _____.
   a. from most to least
   b. from least to most
   c. in no special order

3. Cookies have more sugar than salt. The sugar is listed _____ the salt.
   a. after
   b. below
   c. before

4. Peanut butter made from only peanuts and salt has _____.
   a. fewer peanuts in a serving
   b. more peanuts in a serving
   c. some sugar added to it

5. A label *detective* _____.
   a. reads labels carefully
   b. goes shopping
   c. finds the right aisle

6. A label detective pays attention to _____.
   a. brand names only
   b. the ingredients and the order listed
   c. cost only

PRACTICE

A. Which would you buy? Read the following labels from baby food. Answer the questions about the order of ingredients. The first one is done for you.

> **Baby Food A: Baby's Chicken Dinner**
> ingredients: water, carrots, chicken, potatoes, peas, rice flour, corn, dry milk, wheat flour, oil, flavorings

> **Baby Food B: Baby's Yummy Chicken Surprise**
> ingredients: water, potatoes, rice flour, potato starch, carrots, peas, corn, chicken, dry milk, wheat flour, oil, flavorings

	Baby Food A	B
1. Which ingredient is rice flour?	6th	3rd
2. Which ingredient is chicken?		
3. Which ingredient is carrots?		
4. Which ingredient is potatoes?		

5. Which baby food seems better? Why? _____

_____

_____

B. Label detective at home. Check some food labels at home. Write down the ingredients from five labels. Pay attention to the order of the ingredients. The first one is done for you.

1. __Crackers: wheat flour, shortening, salt, yeast,__

   __sugar__ _____

2. _____

   _____

3. _____

   _____

4. _____

   _____

5. _____

   _____

6. _____

   _____

UNIT 5

Dinner's Ready!

This unit is about:

- making good choices when you are in a hurry

Think About

When you are in a hurry, what do you buy at the market? How do you decide what to buy?

Dinner's Ready!

Marie is at the supermarket. It is six o'clock. She needs to find something fast to cook for dinner. She knows that her children will be hungry. There are so many choices at the store. How does she decide what to buy?

She starts looking in the frozen food **section**. There are a lot of choices! She picks up some TV dinners. As she walks to the check-out counter, she decides to play label detective. She looks at the order of ingredients on the packages. She notices that these complete dinners are mostly mashed potatoes and gravy. There is not much meat. There are not many green vegetables. She also sees many ingredients with long names. She cannot **identify** most of these. She thinks about the four food groups. Maybe the TV dinners are not the best choice. She is paying mostly for mashed potatoes and gravy.

Marie wants to find something that tastes good, is easy to cook, and is good for her family. She knows some packaged foods are better than others. She thinks about the four food groups. Finally, she decides to buy frozen fish sticks, a box of macaroni and cheese, and some peas.

She walks through the store. She reads the labels on different products. She checks the labels and prices on the boxes of macaroni and cheese. She decides to buy the **store brand**. The ingredients are almost the same as the name brands. But the store brand is a lot cheaper.

Marie does not want to spend a lot of money for something that is not good for her family. She wants the food to taste good. And, she wants something fast and easy.

Marie thinks about the basic food groups as she goes through the store. She decides what to buy. Then, she checks the ingredients and the prices. She knows easy food can be **economical**—or inexpensive—and good for her family, too!

REVIEW

Choose the best answer. Circle it. Go back to the reading to check your answers. The first one is done for you.

1. Marie wants something _____ for dinner.
   a. quick
   b. expensive
   c. difficult

2. Marie _____ to find out the ingredients in the TV dinners.
   a. asks someone
   b. reads the labels
   c. asks her friend

3. The TV dinners do not seem _____ to Marie.
   a. easy
   b. expensive
   c. balanced

4. Marie wants something that tastes good and is _____.
   a. good for her family
   b. a famous name brand
   c. hard to cook

5. The store brand costs _____ than name brands.
   a. more
   b. less
   c. the same

6. Another way to say *economical* is _____.
   a. inexpensive
   b. expensive
   c. easy

PRACTICE

A. Choose the correct word. Complete each sentence with a word from the list. Write the word in the blank. The first one is done for you.

choices	economical	good
picks up	store brand	tastes

1. It is important to try to be __economical__ when we shop.

2. The _____ is often cheaper.

3. There are a lot of _____ at the grocery store.

4. Marie _____ some TV dinners.

5. Marie wants something that _____ good.

6. Marie also wants something that is _____ for her family.

B. List some quick foods. Find some quick foods at the store. List the foods and their ingredients. One suggestion is done for you.

Name	Ingredients
canned stew	meat, potatoes, carrots, onions, water

C. What would you buy? Think about the basic food groups. Make a list of packaged foods you think are good choices when you need something fast. Explain why. One suggestion is done for you.

1. <u>**Frozen cheese pizza. It is made with cheese,**</u>

    <u>**tomatoes, and bread dough.**</u>

2. _____

    _____

3. _____

    _____

4. _____

    _____

5. _____

    _____

6. _____

    _____

UNIT 6

Keep It Clean

This unit is about:

- keeping food clean

- keeping the kitchen clean

Think About

What do you do to get ready to cook?
Where do you cut up food?
Why is it important to keep the kitchen very clean?

Keep It Clean

Cooking can be fun. But it should also be safe from **germs** that can make you sick. One way to be safe is to keep food and food **preparation** areas safe and clean. This means washing often as you cook. Here are a few rules to follow.

Keep your hands clean. Always wash your hands with hot, soapy water before starting to cook. And wash your hands after you **handle** meat or chicken. Wear gloves if you have a cut on your hand. And if you go to the bathroom, do not forget to wash your hands again.

Wash the food well. Scrub all fruits and vegetables. Some vegetables from the store look clean. They still need to be washed. **Rinse** chicken carefully. Rinsing helps remove germs.

Keep kitchen utensils clean. Wash knives and other **utensils** as you use them. This is especially important if you prepare something that will be cooked and something that will not be cooked. For example, if you cut up some meat, wash the knife with hot, soapy water before you use it to cut up salad vegetables. Or if you prepare meatballs, wash the bowl well before you use it as a serving bowl.

Use two cutting boards. Have two cutting boards. Use one for meat, chicken, and fish. Use the other for fruits, vegetables, and other non-meat foods. If you use the same cutting board, germs can move from the meat to the fruits and vegetables. Using two cutting boards reduces **contamination**—or spreading germs.

Clean preparation areas. Keep the area where you are cooking very clean. Be sure to clean it after cutting up meat. Wipe up **spills** right away. Throw out **food scraps** to avoid attracting insects. Insects can carry germs.

It is important to keep the kitchen very clean. A clean kitchen is easier to work in. It is a lot safer, too.

REVIEW

Choose the best answer. Circle it. Go back to the reading to check your answers. The first one is done for you.

1. The first rule in the kitchen is _____.
    a. have fun
    b. keep your hands clean
    c. work fast

2. Before using fruits and vegetables, _____ them.
    a. wash
    b. taste
    c. cook

3. After cutting up meat, _____.
    a. throw away the cutting board
    b. it is not important to wash the cutting board and knife
    c. wash your hands, knife, and preparation area

4. Using two cutting boards is _____.
    a. more economical
    b. faster
    c. safer

5. Wiping up spills is an example of _____.
    a. keeping the area clean
    b. using two cutting boards
    c. scrubbing fruits and vegetables

6. Another title for this reading could be _____.
    a. How to Shop for Food
    b. How to Cook Chicken
    c. A Clean Kitchen Is Safer

PRACTICE

A. What would you say? The people below do not have good cooking habits. What would you tell them to do differently? Write your answers on the lines below. The first one is done for you.

1. Thomas wakes up late. He cuts his hand making breakfast. He runs into work, takes off his jacket, and starts cutting up vegetables right away.

   <u>**He should wash his hands and wear gloves.**</u>

   _____

2. Ann is in a hurry. She takes a chicken from her grocery bag and throws it right into a pot on the stove.

   _____

   _____

3. Theresa spills some sugar. She leaves it on the counter.

   _____

   _____

4. Carl uses the same knife to cut up meat and then the salad vegetables.

   _____

   _____

B. Vocabulary practice. Complete each sentence with a word from the list. Write the word in the blank. The first one is done for you.

contamination	gloves	handling
rinsing	soapy	utensil

1. Using two cutting boards reduces __**contamination**__ .

2. Use hot, _____ water to wash your hands.

3. Wash your hands after _____ uncooked chicken.

4. Wear _____ if you have a cut.

5. _____chicken helps remove germs.

6. A knife is a kitchen _____ .

C. What would you do? You are going to cook a chicken. What should you do first? What should you do next? The first step is marked for you. Put the other steps in the right order.

1. Wash your hands with hot, soapy water.   __1__

2. Cut the chicken on a cutting board.   _____

3. Finally, wash your hands again.   _____

4. Wash the cutting board with soap and water.   _____

5. Rinse the chicken carefully.   _____

UNIT 7

Store It Right!

This unit is about:

- storing food

- using the refrigerator wisely

Think About

Why is it important to put food in the refrigerator?
What do you do with any food left after dinner?
How can you tell if milk has "gone bad?"

37

Store It Right!

You already know that it is important to keep everything in the kitchen clean. It is also important to be organized as you cook. You need to be organized about **storing** food correctly, too.

Food can **spoil**. Food that is spoiled is not good to eat. Food that is spoiled may look or smell different. It usually does not taste good. More important, it is not safe to eat. Spoiled food can make you very sick.

If something looks or smells spoiled, do not eat it. Some people say, "When in doubt, throw it out." This means if something does not seem okay to eat, throw it away. It is better to be safe than sorry with spoiled food.

How can you keep food from spoiling? The best way is to keep foods cold. Meats, dairy products, and vegetables spoil very quickly. Put them in the refrigerator as soon as you buy them. Don't add new milk to old milk. It can all go bad. Put meat in the freezer if you do not plan to use it right away. Uncooked meat should not be left in the refrigerator more than two or three days. It should be put in the freezer.

Cooked food will not last forever. It should be **refrigerated** as soon as possible. Never leave food out **overnight**. Food left out on the stove can spoil in just a few hours. Store the food in clean **containers**. And cover it well before putting it in the refrigerator. Plan to use up **leftovers** within a few days. Clear out the refrigerator regularly.

Store food properly to keep it from spoiling. Know what you have and by when it has to be used. And remember, if any food looks or smells funny, don't eat it.

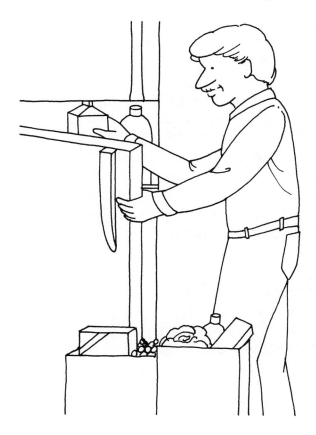

REVIEW

Choose the best answer. Circle it. Go back to the reading to check your answers. The first one is done for you.

1. Food that is spoiled is _____.
    a. safe to eat
    b. probably still okay to eat
    (c.) not safe to eat

2. Spoiled food often _____.
    a. smells different
    b. tastes good
    c. is safe

3. You are *in doubt* about some food. To you, the food seems _____.
    a. spoiled
    b. okay to eat
    c. good for you

4. Uncooked meat you don't plan to eat right away _____.
    a. will not spoil if left out
    b. will be okay in the refrigerator for a week or two
    c. should be put in the freezer

5. Cooked food _____.
    a. may be left out
    b. must be refrigerated
    c. will usually not spoil

6. Cooked food in the refrigerator needs to be _____.
    a. left out instead
    b. used within a few days
    c. left uncovered

PRACTICE

A. What is wrong with this kitchen? Look at the picture. There are five things wrong. What are they? Write your answers on the lines. The first one is done for you.

1.   **There is a carton of milk on the counter.**

2. _____

3. _____

4. _____

5. _____

B. What do you suggest? What other things could you do to make your kitchen a better place to work? List your ideas below. One suggestion is given.

___Keep the counter clean,___

_____

_____

_____

C. Do or don't? Decide if you should or should not do the things listed below. Put a check in the box under **Do** or **Don't** to make each sentence correct. The first one is done for you.

Do	Don't	
	√	Eat spoiled food.
		Eat strange-smelling food.
		Throw away food that looks strange.
		Put food in the refrigerator.
		Leave cooked food out overnight.
		Use clean storage containers.
		Cover food well.
		Store leftovers a long time.

UNIT 8

A Cold?
No, Thanks!

This unit is about:

- how someone gets a cold

- how to keep from giving a cold to others

Think About

Do you get colds often?
How do you feel when you have a cold?
What do you do to stay healthy?

A Cold? No, Thanks!

Luisa works in the kitchen at a restaurant. One day, she wakes up with a runny nose. She is sneezing and coughing. She has a cold. Luisa calls her boss to say she is sick. They both decide she should not go to work. They know that colds are easy to **spread** from person to person. They do not want anyone else to get Luisa's cold.

How do colds spread? You get a cold from germs. The type of germ that gives you a cold is called a **virus**. This virus travels easily from person to person. Whenever you cough or sneeze, the virus **sprays**, or shoots out, into the air. Even if you cover your mouth, the virus gets on your hands. In fact, your hands are the main way a cold is spread. The virus spreads to whatever you touch: food, dishes, glasses, and other people.

If you get a cold, how can you keep from spreading it to others? Luisa stayed at home in bed to rest for two days. She did not see anyone.

When Luisa went back to work she was very careful. She covered her mouth whenever she sneezed or coughed. She washed her hands after she sneezed or coughed or blew her nose. She washed everything she used, such as kitchen utensils, before someone else used them.

Luisa got over her cold after a few days. Now she tries to avoid catching colds from other people. She washes her hands before preparing food at home and at work. She tries to keep from getting too close to someone who has a cold. She keeps her hands away from her nose and mouth.

Luisa also stays healthy by eating well and getting enough rest. She eats lots of fruit, such as oranges and apples. She does not stay up late.

Luisa is saying "No thanks" to getting another cold. If you get a cold, try not to spread it. Wash your hands often. To avoid getting another cold, take good care of yourself.

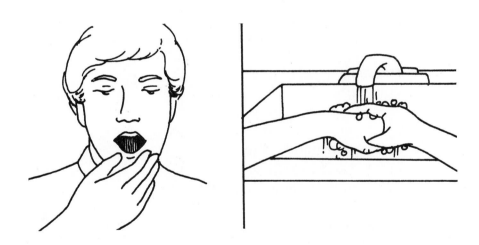

REVIEW

Choose the best answer. Circle it. Go back to the reading to check your answers. The first one is done for you.

1. You get a cold from _____.
    a. bad food
    b. a virus
    c. being in a cold room

2. A virus can move from person to person _____.
    a. in a sneeze
    b. from soap and water
    c. in the rain

3. When you cover your mouth, the virus _____.
    a. spreads into the air
    b. goes onto your hand
    c. cannot travel anywhere

4. Colds are spread mainly by _____.
    a. touching things
    b. sneezing
    c. coughing

5. One way to avoid catching a cold is to _____.
    a. wash your hands often
    b. cover your mouth
    c. touch your nose and mouth

6. People can stay healthy by _____.
    a. eating only fruits and water
    b. staying away from friends and family
    c. eating well and getting rest

PRACTICE

A. Yes or no? Decide if you should or should not do the things listed below. Put a check under **YES** or **NO**. The first one is done for you.

1. You have a cold. What should you do?

	YES	NO
cover your mouth when you sneeze	√	
visit friends		
rest		
stay up late		

2. You want to avoid getting a cold.
    What should you do?

	YES	NO
visit friends who are sick		√
keep your hands near your mouth		
get plenty of rest		
eat right		
avoid washing your hands		

B. What do you do? After you catch a cold, you cannot really make it go away faster. You can do things to feel better, though. When you have a cold, what do you do? Write your ideas on the blank lines below. One idea is already given.

Drink lots of tea with honey and lemon.

_____

_____

_____

C. Go to work or stay home? All of the people below have bad colds. Give a reason why each person should or should not go to work. Write your ideas on the lines. The first one is done for you.

1. a cook   __A cook has to touch other people's__

   __food. A cook should probably stay home.__

   _____

2. a carpenter _____

   _____

   _____

3. a teacher _____

   _____

   _____

4. a police officer _____

   _____

   _____

5. a waiter or waitress _____

   _____

   _____

6. a meat cutter _____

   _____

   _____

UNIT 9

A Healthy Mouth

This unit is about:

- caring for your teeth

Think About

What do you do to take care of your teeth?
How often do you go to the dentist?

A Healthy Mouth

Angela works as a hostess at a small restaurant. She sees and talks to customers—the people who eat at the restaurant—every day. She wants to look her best and to have clean, fresh breath. She also wants to take good care of herself. Part of taking care of herself is taking care of her teeth.

Angela takes care of her teeth by going to a dental clinic every six months. A **dental hygienist** cleans Angela's teeth. After the cleaning, a dentist checks her teeth and gums. Angela is always happy when she does not have any **cavities,** or small holes in her teeth.

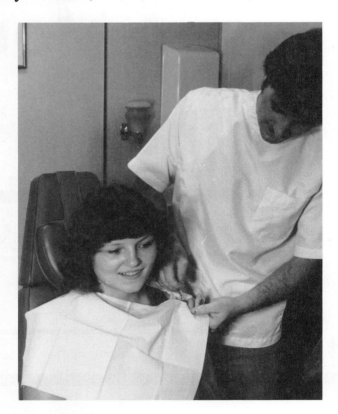

The last time Angela went to the dental clinic, the dental hygienist talked to Angela about good habits. She told Angela that one way to keep from getting cavities was to **floss** her teeth. The hygienist gave Angela a free sample of floss. She showed Angela how to pull the thin thread of floss between her teeth. Flossing teeth after brushing removes food stuck between teeth. It also removes **plaque**, a white material that harms your teeth and gums. Flossing helps to keep teeth clean and gums healthy.

Before Angela left, the hygienist gave her a **booklet** to read. The booklet was about caring for teeth. The booklet said to avoid eating sweet foods, especially between meals. The sugar in sweet foods can cause cavities. If it is hard to brush teeth at work, drink some water or eat an apple. An apple is not as good as a toothbrush. But an apple will clean the teeth a little.

The booklet showed Angela how to teach her children good habits. Even small children can brush and floss their teeth. It can be a game for them. Angela cannot brush her baby's teeth. But she can give him good food. She can also avoid letting him fall asleep with a bottle in his mouth. The milk in the bottle may drip after the baby is asleep. The sugar in the milk can hurt the baby's teeth.

The last thing that the booklet suggested was to go to the dentist regularly. The booklet listed the different places to go: a dental clinic, a private dentist, or a dental school clinic. A private dentist sees patients in an office and is usually more expensive than a clinic. A dental school is part of a college where people learn to be dentists. Dental schools often have clinics where dental students take care of your teeth. A dental school clinic is less expensive than a private dentist.

Some people are afraid of dentists. They are afraid the dentist will hurt them, so they do not go regularly. They wait until a tooth hurts. Actually, it hurts more if you wait. A small problem becomes a big problem. Big problems usually hurt more and cost more to take care of. Angela has learned that taking care of her teeth means going to the dentist regularly. She has good dental care habits and teaches them to her children.

REVIEW

Choose the best answer. Circle it. Go back to the reading to check your answers. The first one is done for you.

1. Angela is happy when she _____.
   a. has no cavities
   b. has some cavities
   c. does not take care of her teeth

2. After eating something sweet, _____ if you cannot brush right away.
   a. have a cookie
   b. eat an apple
   c. your teeth will be clean

3. Flossing your teeth _____.
   a. is a bad habit
   b. removes plaque
   c. is bad for the gums

4. A small problem in a tooth _____.
   a. should not be brushed
   b. is not important
   c. can get bigger

5. Dental school clinics are _____ than private dentists.
   a. less expensive
   b. more expensive
   c. a lot more expensive

6. Another title for this reading could be _____.
   a. Food for Strong Teeth
   b. Keep Your Teeth Healthy
   c. How to Brush Your Teeth

PRACTICE

A. Do or don't? Decide if you should or should not do the things listed below. Put a check in the box under **Do** or **Don't** to make each sentence correct. The first one is done for you.

Do	Don't	
√		Brush your teeth after every meal.
		Eat a lot of candy and sugar.
		Let a baby fall asleep with a bottle.
		Floss your teeth every day.
		Avoid going to the dentist.
		Wait until a problem gets big.
		Have the hygienist clean your teeth.
		Go to the dentist regularly.

B. Choose a word. Complete each sentence with a word or phrase from the group below. Write the answer in the space. The first one is done for you.

avoid	**booklet**	**checked**
habit	**hurt**	**meal**

1. The dentist __checked_____ Angela's teeth.

2. Angela read the _____ about caring for teeth.

3. Try to _____ sweet foods.

4. Brush after every _____.

5. Some people think dentists will _____ them.

6. Flossing every day is a good _____.

C. Write some rules. Write some rules to follow if you want to have healthy teeth and gums. Some words are given to write rules about. The first one is done for you.

	Rules for a Healthy Mouth
Cavities	**Brush and floss teeth so you won't get cavities.**
Sweet foods	
Baby bottles	
Water	
Brush	
Floss	
Dentist	

UNIT 10

Kitchen Safety

This unit is about:

- keeping kitchens safe

- kitchen safety for children

Think About

What are some dangers in the kitchen?
What is especially dangerous for children?
What do you do to make your kitchen safe?

Kitchen Safety

Two-year-old Thomas and his mother were in the kitchen. The phone rang in the living room. Thomas's mother ran to answer it. Thomas went to the stove and pulled the handle of a pot of spaghetti sauce. The hot sauce spilled on him and burned him badly.

Kids want to see and try everything. They are curious. Children learn by looking, touching, and trying things. But this can be a problem. There are many things that children should not touch or do. More accidents happen in the home than anywhere else. And the kitchen can be the most dangerous place. How can you keep your kitchen safe? Here are a few things to do:

- Keep the handles of pots and pans turned inward where children cannot reach them.

- Never leave food cooking on the stove **unattended**. A child might get curious and pull a chair to the stove to see what is cooking. And, of course, the food might burn.

- Wipe up spills right away. No one wants to slip and fall!

- Keep sharp knives in a rack, not a drawer, so they are out of children's reach.

- Keep **bleach**, **detergent**, and other cleaning supplies where children cannot get them. Be sure to leave them in the containers they came in. Someone might not know that bleach is bleach if it is in a milk carton. If you must change the container, label it carefully.

- Don't use **extension cords** with electrical **appliances**. Toasters and coffee pots are made with very short cords to be safe. A long cord makes it easy to pull the appliance off the counter.

- Put child locks on cabinets that you do not want children to get into. Child locks are easy for adults to open but not for kids.

The kitchen is often a place where the family spends time together. It can be a happy place. It can also be a dangerous place. Children are curious. The kitchen is full of things children want to explore. Keeping the kitchen safe is important.

REVIEW

Choose the best answer. Circle it. Go back to the reading to check your answers. The first one is done for you.

1. Did Thomas's mother have the handle turned inward?
    a. Yes
    b. I think so.
    c. I don't think so.

2. People can _____ on spills.
    a. reach
    b. slip
    c. pull

3. The best place for sharp knives is _____.
    a. in a rack
    b. in a drawer
    c. on a shelf

4. Cleaning supplies _____.
    a. are not usually dangerous
    b. should be left in the containers they come in
    c. should not be used in the house

5. Why do appliances have short cords? To make them _____.
    a. easier to pull
    b. more dangerous
    c. safer

6. The main idea of this reading is _____.
    a. pots and pans are dangerous
    b. the kitchen can be a safe place
    c. children should not be in the kitchen

PRACTICE

A. Kitchen safety. Look at the picture below carefully. Notice what safety rules are being broken. Write down some ways to make this kitchen safer. The first one is done for you.

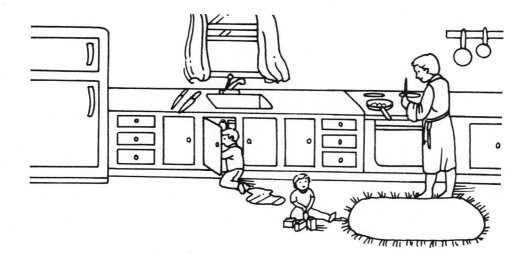

1. __Turn the handle of the pan inward.__

2. _____

3. _____

4. _____

5. _____

B. Why is it dangerous? Read the following situations. Think about the kitchen safety rules and explain why these situations are dangerous. The first one is done for you.

1. Singu left some soup cooking while he ran to the post office.

   _**A fire could start.**_____

2. Maria often leaves the handles of her pots sticking out.

   _____

3. Thomas keeps sharp knives in the same drawer as his forks and spoons.

   _____

4. Margo puts bleach in soda bottles because it is easier to pour.

   _____

5. Alex uses an extension cord for his coffee pot. He likes to keep it on the kitchen table.

   _____

C. Take a look around. Think about your own kitchen. What could you do to make it a safer place? Write your ideas. One suggestion is given.

1. _**Put child locks on my cabinets.**_____

2. _____

3. _____

4. _____

5. _____

UNIT 11

Fire in the Kitchen

This unit is about:

- preventing fires in the kitchen

Think About

Has anything in your kitchen ever caught fire?
When? What happened? What did you do?
What are some ways to prevent fires?

Fire in the Kitchen

Theresa threw on her bathrobe and went to the kitchen to cook breakfast. As she stood at the stove fixing some fried eggs, she noticed a funny smell. Before she knew it, the sleeve of her bathrobe was on fire. She ran to the sink and stuck her arm under the cold water. Luckily, she was not hurt.

Catching on fire like that scared Theresa. As she ate her breakfast, she looked around the kitchen. No one wants a fire in the kitchen. Yet, the kitchen is a place where fires can happen easily.

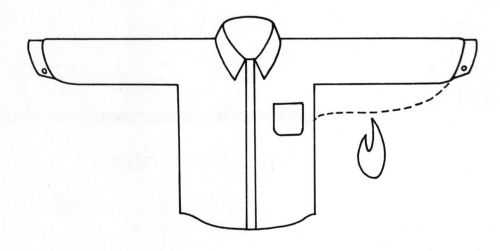

On her way home from work, Theresa stopped off at the fire station. On the wall of the fire station there was a chart. The chart was about **fire prevention** in the kitchen. She got a copy of the chart to take home.

Kitchen items	Safety Rules
Matches	Never leave matches on the stove or anywhere children can reach.
Clothes	Don't wear clothes with loose sleeves when you cook. This is especially important for clothes made of **synthetic**, or man-made, materials.
Curtains	Don't hang curtains near the stove. They can catch fire easily.
Grease	Don't leave hot grease unattended. And, wipe up any grease on the stove. Grease fires are very dangerous.
Baking soda	Keep baking soda nearby to put out a grease fire.
Grills	Don't use a charcoal or gas grill in the house. A grill can get knocked over and the fire can spread. Also, these grills use up oxygen. They need proper **ventilation**.
Smoke detector	Check the battery regularly. Don't **disconnect** it. It can tell you quickly if there is a fire in the house.

By following these rules, Theresa can make her kitchen a safer place.

REVIEW

Choose the best answer. Circle it. Go back to the reading to check your answers. The first one is done for you.

1. Theresa's robe caught fire as she _____.
    a. threw on her robe
    (b.) fried some eggs
    c. went to the kitchen

2. Theresa got a fire prevention chart _____.
    a. at work
    b. at home
    c. at the fire station

3. Loose sleeves are _____ when you cook.
    a. dangerous
    b. big
    c. synthetic

4. Another way to say *don't leave hot grease unattended* is _____.
    a. leave hot grease alone
    b. don't watch hot grease
    c. don't leave hot grease alone

5. We can use _____ to put out grease fires.
    a. baking soda
    b. grills
    c. grease

6. Another title for this reading could be _____.
    a. Don't Wear Loose Sleeves
    b. Prevent Kitchen Fires
    c. Use Your Smoke Detector

PRACTICE

A. Do or don't? Decide if you should or should not do the things listed below to have a safe kitchen. Put a check in the box under **Do** or **Don't**. The first one is done for you.

Do	Don't	
	√	Leave matches on the stove.
		Wipe up grease on the stove.
		Pay attention to the clothes you wear.
		Watch hot oil carefully.
		Hang curtains near the stove.
		Disconnect the smoke detector.
		Always have some baking soda.
		Use a charcoal grill indoors.

B. Say it another way. Read the following sentences. For each sentence, look at the *italicized* word. Write the sentence a different way. Use a word from the reading. The first one is done for you.

1. Theresa *put on* her robe.

   Theresa threw on her robe.

2. Theresa was *cooking* some fried eggs.

   _____

3. She *put* her arm under the cold water.

   _____

4. Theresa was *frightened*.

_____

5. The chart was about *keeping fires from happening*.

_____

6. Nylon is a *man-made* material.

_____

C. What would you suggest? Read the following situations. Explain why these people should not do what they do. The first one is done for you.

1. Walter always leaves his stove covered with grease.

   He should clean it. It is not safe.

2. Sonja usually wears a loose robe when she cooks breakfast.

   _____

3. Vim keeps his matches in a box on the stove.

   _____

4. Kim just bought long nylon curtains for the window above his stove.

   _____

5. Horacio took the battery out of his smoke detector. He doesn't like the sound it makes when the battery is low.

   _____

First Aid First

This unit is about:

- first aid for cuts and burns

- what is in a first-aid kit

Think About

When was the last time you cut or burned yourself?
What did you do?
Did you feel helpless or calm?

First Aid First

Roger is cooking dinner. He cuts his finger as he chops carrots. Brenda has boiled some potatoes. She drains the water and the pot slips. Boiling water covers her hand. She cries out in pain. These kinds of accidents happen every day. What can you do to help if someone gets hurt?

Learn basic **first aid**. First aid is the care you give when someone first gets hurt. What you do or don't do those first few minutes after an injury is important. You can help another person by knowing first aid. You can also help yourself with first aid if you have an injury when you are alone.

The most common kinds of injuries in the kitchen are cuts and burns. Unless a cut or burn is serious, the first aid for these is fairly easy. For a simple burn, cold water is enough. Hold the burned area under cold water until the pain goes away (about ten minutes). Dry carefully. Do not use vaseline, **salve**, or grease. These oils will keep air from getting to the burn and will slow healing. Leave the burn uncovered or cover with a dry gauze bandage.

For a simple cut, it is usually enough to clean the cut and use a bandage. If the bleeding does not stop right away, you need to do two things: apply **pressure** to the cut and **elevate** it. To apply pressure, use a clean cloth or bandage and press down on the cut. Keep the cut elevated, or raised, until the bleeding stops.

Sometimes, the injury may be more serious. It may be a deep cut that will not stop bleeding. Or it may be a bad burn. Give first aid to the person hurt and then take them to the doctor. If this is not possible, give first aid and then call for medical help. Medical help will come quickly and can take the injured person to a hospital.

Knowing first aid can help you to stay calm. It will also help calm the person who is hurt. And it may save someone's life.

A first-aid kit. Everyone should have medical supplies or a first-aid kit. Below is a list of basic supplies that you should have. The chart tells you what to use each item for. For example, adhesive tape is used to hold bandages in place.

Supplies	Use
gauze bandages	to clean cuts and to cover cuts and burns
adhesive tape	to hold bandages
bandages	to cover small cuts
soap	to clean cuts
rubbing alcohol	to kill germs
scissors	to cut gauze and tape
matches	to **sterilize** (or clean) pins and other things
aspirin	for fever or aches

Be prepared. Keep your first-aid supplies in one place and keep them clean. Make sure you understand how to use them. Many hospitals and evening schools teach first aid. To find out about taking a class, call a local hospital. First aid is important for everyone to know.

REVIEW

Choose the best answer. Circle it. Go back to the reading to check your answer. The first one is done for you.

1. You help someone who is hurt. This is _____.
   a. a supply
   b. a kit
   c. first aid

2. Cuts and burns are common _____ in the kitchen.
   a. germs
   b. injuries
   c. supplies

3. The best treatment for a simple burn is _____.
   a. salve
   b. cold water
   c. a bandage

4. When you elevate your arm, you _____.
   a. wash it
   b. apply direct pressure
   c. raise it

5. First-aid supplies should be kept _____.
   a. cold and dry
   b. clean and together in one place
   c. next to bandages

6. Another title for this reading could be _____.
   a. Be Prepared
   b. Emergencies at Work
   c. Falling Down the Stairs

PRACTICE

A. Choose the correct word. Look at the words below. Choose the best word for each sentence and write it in the space. The first one is done for you.

> clean   elevate   first aid
> pressure   water

1. Give __first aid__ right after someone is hurt.

2. Put cold _____ on a simple burn.

3. _____ a cut, then put on a bandage.

4. Sometimes you can stop the bleeding by applying _____

_____ .

5. If you _____, or raise, a cut the bleeding may slow down.

B. What would you suggest? Read the following problems. Decide what you would do to help the person. The first one is done for you.

1. Dori got a small cut on her finger.

   __I would wash the cut and put a bandage on it.__

2. Jose spilled boiling soup on his arm.

   _____

3. Vim cut his thumb. It is bleeding a lot.

   _____

4. Your friend has cut himself. He is very scared.

_____

C. Read about the first-aid course. This hospital has sent information about first-aid courses. Read the information. Then, answer the questions. The first one is done for you.

South End Hospital
14 Broadway, Rockaway, NY

325-2550

We are pleased to offer free first-aid classes. Below is a description of each with the days and times. If you are interested in taking any of them, please call Special Services at 325-2550. We look forward to seeing you.

First Aid for Beginners:
Learn about common emergencies (cuts, burns, broken bones). Monday & Wednesday 6:30-9:00pm.

Advanced First Aid:
Learn about head injuries, choking, heart attacks, and bandaging. Tuesday & Thursday 6:30-9:00pm.

Water Safety:
Learn about problems and emergencies that happen near the water - how to prevent and handle them. Wednesday 6:00-9:00pm.

Child Safety:
Learn what problems and situations are common for children. Monday 7:00-9:30pm.

---

1. Where are the courses taught? __at South End Hospital__

2. How much do the courses cost? _____

3. If you have not taken a first-aid course before, which one

   would be good to take first? _____

4. Which course teaches you about water emergencies? _____

   _____

5. Which course meets on Monday night? _____

6. Which course teaches about head injuries? _____

   _____

For Cooking, Not Heating

This unit is about:

- using a gas stove

- safety rules for using natural gas

Think About

How do you heat your home?
What do you do if the heat stops working?
Why do you think gas has a funny smell?

For Cooking, Not Heating

Vince came back to his apartment late one winter night. It was so cold! He turned on his kitchen oven to warm the apartment up quickly. He lay down on the couch and waited to get warm. The next thing he knew, it was 2 a.m. He woke up suddenly. There was a strong smell of gas in his apartment. He went to the kitchen. The flame had gone out. Gas was filling his apartment!

Many people use natural gas every day. Gas is an example of a **utility**. Utilities are public services. Other utilities are electricity, water, and phone service. Natural gas is easy to use and safe when used correctly. But you have to use it correctly. A kitchen stove is for cooking, not heating. Heating with a gas kitchen stove is dangerous.

In Vince's case, the flame went out. Gas was filling his apartment. Vince was lucky to wake up in time and get out of the apartment. Even if the flame does not go out, it is still dangerous. Burning gas uses up the oxygen in the room. It produces **carbon monoxide**. Over time, the carbon monoxide can build up and become dangerous.

Gas is safe and easy to use, but you have to be careful. Gas has a smell. The gas company gives it that funny smell so that we will **recognize** it. We will know if gas is leaking.

If you smell gas in your home, do not ignore it. First, check the **pilot light** on the stove. It might have gone out. Quickly open the doors and windows. Then, call the gas company. Call from a neighbor's house or from a pay phone. Do not call from your own phone. Also, do not strike a match or light a cigarette. Do not turn the lights on or off. The telephone or the lights could release a **spark**. The spark could start a fire.

If you need more heat in your home, think about what you can do. Do you rent? Then, talk to the landlord or building manager. Do you own your own home? If so, you have several choices. One thing you can do is to buy an electric space heater.

Kitchen stoves are for cooking, not heating. Sometimes, it may seem like a good idea to use them for heating, especially if it is very cold. But it is not. Gas can be dangerous.

REVIEW

Choose the best answer. Circle it. Go back to the reading to check your answers. The first one is done for you.

1. Vince turned on his oven to _____.
   a. cook a snack
   b. lie down
   (c.) warm up

2. When Vince woke up, _____.
   a. he waited for it to get warm
   b. his apartment was full of gas
   c. he turned on his oven

3. Heating with a kitchen stove is _____.
   a. dangerous
   b. correct
   c. safe

4. A *utility* is _____.
   a. dangerous
   b. for cooking
   c. a public service

5. If there is a gas leak, _____.
   a. strike a match
   b. call the gas company
   c. close the windows and doors

6. The main idea of this reading is _____.
   a. natural gas has a funny smell
   b. don't use kitchen stoves for heating
   c. space heaters are better for heating

PRACTICE

A. Choose a word. Complete each sentence with a word or phrase from the reading. Write the answer in the space. The first one is done for you.

carbon monoxide		dangerous
gas company	recognize	spark

1. Heating with a kitchen stove is **dangerous**_____.

2. Leaking gas is easy to _____.

3. Call the _____ for help.

4. _____ can build up if we use a gas oven for heating.

5. The telephone can release a _____.

B. What should you do first? There is a gas leak in your apartment. What should you do? Below are the steps. Number them in order from 1 to 6. The first one is done for you.

1. Open the doors and windows.   _____

2. Check the pilot light.   _____

3. Call the gas company.   _____

4. You smell some gas.   __1__

5. The pilot light is O.K.   _____

6. Go to a neighbor's house or pay phone. _____

C. What do you suggest? No one likes to be cold. What are some things we can do to be warm at home? Write your ideas on the lines below. One suggestion is given.

<u>**Close the curtains at night.**</u>

_____

_____

_____

_____

_____

D. Know those numbers. It is important to know where to call if you have a problem with a utility. Use your local phone book for this activity. Follow the directions and fill in the chart below.

1. Look up the telephone numbers of the utility companies in your area.

2. Check the front of the phone book to see if there is a number in your area to call for help with heating. Try looking under _Heating Assistance_. What is the number?

Utility	Number
electricity	
gas	
sewer	
telephone	
water	

Getting Help When You Need It

This unit is about:

- knowing what to do to get emergency help

- calling 911 or the operator

Think About

Have you ever had to call for emergency help? What happened? What did you do to get help fast?

Have you ever been in an emergency room? What was it like?

Getting Help When You Need It

It is seven o'clock on a Sunday morning. Larry is making pancakes for his parents and sister. He decides to add sliced peaches. He washes and cuts up four peaches. Water and juice drip onto the kitchen floor. Larry reaches for a towel to wipe up his shoes and the wet floor. He slips and falls. Larry falls hard on his right arm. He feels a sharp pain.

Luckily, Larry's father and sister heard him fall and ran to help him. They both felt Larry might have hurt his arm badly. So they drove him to the emergency room at a hospital near their apartment.

At the hospital, a doctor looked at Larry's arm. Larry did not break his arm. But he did sprain it. A nurse put his arm in a sling. Larry will not be able to use his right arm until it heals. But he is lucky. He got help when he needed it.

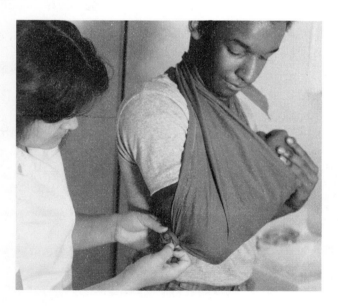

What happens if you do not have a car or live far from a bus stop? You need to call for help then. In most large cities, you can call for help by dialing 911 on the telephone. The **dispatcher**, or person who answers your call, will send an **ambulance**. An ambulance is a special car or van used to move people who are hurt. In the ambulance, there may be an **EMT**, an emergency medical technician. Or there may be a **paramedic**. Paramedics and EMTs have special training in first aid. They can take care of you until the ambulance gets to the hospital.

TO CALL FOR
EMERGENCY SERVICES

911

You can call 911 when you need any kind of emergency help. A dispatcher will send an ambulance, the police, or a fire truck. When you call 911, give the dispatcher the following information:

1. your name
2. your address
3. what the problem is
4. what type of help you need

Don't hang up too soon. Be sure to stay on the line until the dispatcher tells you to hang up.

Some cities and towns do not yet use 911 for emergencies. In those places, you can call the police or dial 0 for the telephone **operator**. The operator will make sure that you get help.

Emergencies happen fast. It is best to know ahead of time how to call for help. You may not have time to look in the phone book for an emergency number. Keep important numbers next to your telephone. Make sure that any children living with you know the numbers, too. That way, you can all get the help you need.

REVIEW

Choose the best answer. Circle it. Go back to the reading to check your answers. The first one is done for you.

1. You can call _____ if there is an emergency.
   a. 411
   (b.) 911
   c. 611

2. In places with no 911, call the _____.
   a. paramedic
   b. nearest neighbor
   c. police

3. It is important to give the 911 operator your _____.
   a. address
   b. age
   c. occupation

4. A _____ works on an ambulance.
   a. phone operator
   b. police officer
   c. paramedic

5. Emergency phone numbers should be kept _____.
   a. near your telephone
   b. at a close friend's house
   c. in a closet

6. Another title for this reading could be _____.
   a. First Aid for Cuts and Burns
   b. How to Call for Emergency Help
   c. People Who Work in the Emergency Room

PRACTICE

A. Did she say the right thing? Read what Mari said when she called a 911 dispatcher. Then, answer the questions. Underline the correct answer. The first one is done for you.

911:    Emergency. What's the matter?
Mari: We need help. There's been an accident!
911:    OK. I need your name.
Mari: Mari Sihng. S-I-H-N-G. My sister fell. Her head is bleeding a lot.
911:    Where are you?
Mari: In the kitchen.
911:    Is your sister conscious? Is she awake?
Mari: Yes, but she's bleeding very bad. Please send someone. I have to help her now. Good-bye.

1. Did Mari give her name?	**YES**	**NO**
2. Did she give the address?	**YES**	**NO**
3. Did she say what the problem was?	**YES**	**NO**
4. Did she say what help she needed?	**YES**	**NO**

B. What should he say? Read the paragraph below. Imagine this person calling 911 for help. Then, on the lines below the paragraph, write down what he should tell the 911 dispatcher.

Stuart Low lives with his family at 231 Kennedy Street, in a second floor apartment. His grandfather has just slipped and fallen in the kitchen. He is holding his hip and groaning. He says he thinks he broke something. He says the pain is terrible. Stuart is afraid to move him for fear of hurting him more. He calls 911.

_____

_____

_____

_____

_____

C. Choose the correct word. Read the following sentences. Choose the best word to fill the space. Write the word in the space. The first one is done for you.

accident   ambulance   emergency room
EMT   operator

1. A man at the restaurant was in an __**accident**_____ .

2. We need an _____ to get him to the hospital.

3. I called the _____ for emergency help.

4. The _____ gave the man first aid.

5. At the _____ a nurse helped him.

D. List your emergency numbers. Emergency numbers should be next to your telephone. Make a list of emergency numbers for you and your family.

Name	Telephone Number
Emergency	911
Doctor	
Ambulance	
Police	
Fire Department	
Hospital	
Parents' work numbers	

UNIT 15

On the Level!

This unit is about:

- measuring things in the kitchen

- common measurements

Think About

How do you usually measure ingredients when you cook?
Do you use measuring spoons and cups?

On the Level!

How much flour do you need in the cookies? How much milk in the pancakes? When we cook, we use different **units of measurement**. *Cup, tablespoon*, and *teaspoon* are examples of units of measurement we use often.

When we cook, we need to measure **accurately**. If a recipe says, "Use 2 teaspoons of salt," we need to use a **standard** measuring spoon. A regular teaspoon may be bigger or smaller than a standard one. And the recipe may not turn out the way you wanted it to.

In cooking, **abbreviations** are often used. Look at the chart below. It gives the abbreviations for some common units of measurement. These are used for measuring liquids, such as water, and dry materials, such as flour. Knowing these abbreviations makes it easier to read recipes and to follow the directions on packages of food such as instant soup.

Abbreviations	
teaspoon	tsp.
tablespoon	Tbl. or tbsp.
cup	c.
pint	pt.
quart	qt.
gallon	gal.
ounce	oz.

The next chart shows the **equivalents** of some of these units of measurement. For example, the directions on a can of soup might say, "Add one cup of water." That would be the same as, or equivalent to, adding eight ounces of water.

Equivalents		
3 teaspoons (tsp.)	=	1 tablespoon (Tbl. or tbsp.)
2 tablespoons	=	1 ounce (oz.)
4 tablespoons	=	1/4 cup
5 1/3 tablespoons	=	1/3 cup
1 cup (c.)	=	8 ounces
16 tablespoons	=	1 cup
2 cups	=	1 pint (pt.)
2 pints	=	1 quart (qt.)
4 quarts	=	1 gallon (gal.)

It is important to know the equivalents. Suppose you need to measure 1/3 cup of oil. You cannot find a measuring cup, but you have measuring spoons. If you know that 5 1/3 tablespoons = 1/3 cup, you can measure accurately using the spoons instead.

Use these units of measurement often. We use them in many places besides the kitchen. Knowing these units of measurement and the equivalents is very useful in our daily lives.

REVIEW

Choose the best answer. Circle it. Go back to the reading to check your answers. The first one is done for you.

1. A standard measurement is _____.
   a. bigger
   (b.) accurate
   c. smaller

2. One cup and eight ounces are _____.
   a. exact abbreviations
   b. approximate amounts
   c. equivalent terms

3. We use the abbreviation *pt.* for _____.
   a. pint
   b. pound
   c. teaspoon

4. We use the abbreviation *Tbl.* for _____.
   a. teaspoon
   b. teaspoons
   c. tablespoon

5. The equivalent of *4 Tbl.* is _____.
   a. 1/2 c.
   b. 1/4 c.
   c. 1/3 c.

6. Knowing abbreviations makes it easier to understand _____.
   a. newspapers
   b. recipes
   c. books

PRACTICE

A. Choose a word. Complete each sentence with a word or phrase from the list below. Write the answer in the space. The first one is done for you.

2 Tbl.	abbreviations	accurately
cup	equivalent	tablespoon

1. A __cup__ is a unit of measurement.

2. It is important to measure _____ .

3. _____ are often used in directions on packages.

4. Two measurements that are _____ are the same.

5. One ounce is the same as _____ .

6. A_____ is bigger than a teaspoon.

B. What does it stand for? Abbreviations are used in many places. Look at the abbreviations on the right. In each space, write out the measurement. An example is given for you.

1. __three cups of flour__   3 c. flour

2. _____   2 pt. juice

3. _____   4 oz. water

4. _____   2 qt. milk

5. _____   1 Tbl. oil

6. _____   2 tsp. salt

7. _____   3 tbsp. sugar

8. _____   3 gal. honey

C. What is it the same as? Knowing the equivalents helps us. Look at the measurements on the right. In each space, write out an equivalent measurement. An example is given for you.

1. __1 gallon of milk__   4 qt. milk

2. _____   16 Tbl. oil

3. _____   1/4 c. butter

4. _____   3 tsp. salt

5. _____   2 c. milk

6. _____   4 c. juice

D. At the grocery store. Look at five different products at the store. Look for the package weight on the label of each product. In column **A**, write the name of the product. In column **B**, write how much it contains. An example is given for you.

	A Name of product	B Contents
1.	corn flakes	9 oz. (nine ounces)
2.	_____	_____
3.	_____	_____
4.	_____	_____
5.	_____	_____
6.	_____	_____

More or Less

This unit is about:

- the energy in food

- paying attention to how food is prepared

Think About

What kinds of activities did you do yesterday? Did you walk to the bus stop? Did you swim? Make a list. What did you eat yesterday? Make another list.

More or Less

We have learned that paying attention to the basic food groups is important. We know a balanced diet helps keep us strong and healthy. Along with what we eat, we need to pay attention to how much we eat. If we eat more than we need, we gain weight. If we eat less than we need, we lose weight.

When we think about what to eat, we need to consider calories. **Calories** are the amount of energy in food. We each have our own calorie **requirements**. These requirements depend on our age, our activities, and the kind of work we do. For example, the **elderly**—or older people—usually need to eat less than younger adults. But, growing children need more calories than adults. People who do hard **physical** labor, such as construction workers, need more calories than office workers.

When we decide to eat something, it is good to think about two things: (1) what food group it belongs to, and (2) how many calories it has. Foods have very different amounts of calories. For example, a large bowl of salad may have only 125 calories. A tiny piece of cheesecake may have 450 calories!

How foods are prepared also affects the number of calories. A scrambled egg has 110 calories; a soft-boiled egg has only 80. French fries have about 250 calories a serving; a baked potato with butter has about 125 calories. One cup of sweetened applesauce has 230 calories. One cup of unsweetened applesauce has only 100 calories. Compare the calories in the two breakfasts below.

Breakfast A		Breakfast B	
1 scrambled egg	110	1 soft-boiled egg	80
2 slices bacon	100	2 slices toast with	
1 danish pastry	240	butter	180
1 banana	85	1 slice melon	30
coffee with		black coffee	0
cream and sugar	35		
Total calories	560	Total calories	290

Which breakfast has more calories? Where do the extra calories come from? For example, a scrambled egg made with butter and milk has 30 extra calories. So a person who needs a higher caloric **intake** might choose Breakfast A. A person who needs to lower caloric intake might choose Breakfast B.

Many people do not think about calories. They do not think about how their food is prepared. But the way food is prepared affects how many calories it has. When you are hungry, think about the basic food groups. And think about your energy needs. Are you doing physical labor or exercise? Then you need extra calories. Are you sitting at a desk or relaxing at home? If so, you need fewer calories. If we pay attention to nutrition and calories, we may have healthier lives.

REVIEW

Choose the best answer. Circle it. Go back to the reading to check your answers. The first one is done for you.

1. If we eat too much, we _____.
    a. lose weight
    (b.) gain weight
    c. pay attention to our weight

2. Older people need _____ children.
    a. fewer calories than
    b. more calories than
    c. the same number of calories as

3. Another way to say *calories* is _____.
    a. the food we eat
    b. how much we eat
    c. the amount of energy in food

4. A scrambled egg has _____ a boiled egg.
    a. fewer calories than
    b. more calories than
    c. the same number of calories as

5. If you were working in construction, _____ would be better.
    a. Breakfast B
    b. Breakfast A
    c. either Breakfast A or B

6. How food is prepared can affect _____.
    a. how many calories it has
    b. the basic food groups
    c. our calorie needs

PRACTICE

A. What difference does it make? The chart below shows the number of calories in some foods. Notice how the number of calories changes for each type of food. Answer the questions that follow. The first one is done for you.

FOOD and CALORIES	
1 medium potato, baked	90
1 serving mashed potatoes with milk	125
1 serving french fries	250
1 serving corn flakes, plain	100
1 serving corn flakes, sugar-coated	155
1 serving canned peaches, heavy syrup	90
1 serving canned peaches, light syrup	38
1 fresh peach	35
1 slice of toast, plain	60
butter for toast	35
strawberry jam for toast	55
1 chicken breast, no skin, baked	115
1 chicken breast, fried	155
1 serving canned corn, regular kernel	70
1 serving canned corn, cream style	100

1. How many calories does a serving of plain corn flakes have?

   __100__ **calories**

2. How many more calories does a serving of sugar-coated corn flakes have? _____

3. If you want a potato for dinner, which kind has the most calories? _____

4. Compare the canned peaches. How many *more* calories do peaches in heavy syrup have? _____

5. Which type of chicken breast has 155 calories?

   _____

6. Look at the corn. Which has more calories, cream-style or regular kernel? _____

7. How many calories does a slice of plain toast have?

   _____

8. How many calories are in a slice of toast with butter and jam?

   _____

B. You decide. Think about your daily activities. Think about what you usually eat. Do you eat more than you need to? Do you eat less than you need to? Do you eat enough high-energy food? How could you change your eating habits? Write your ideas on the lines below. One idea is given.

__I could eat fewer french fries._____

_____

_____

_____

_____

_____

_____

96

UNIT 17

Keeping Fit

This unit is about:

- exercising for health

Think About

What do you enjoy doing for exercise?
Where can you exercise?
How do you feel after you exercise?

Keeping Fit

Exercise sounds like work to some people. Just thinking about it makes them tired. They would rather watch sports on TV than play sports themselves.

But, you can feel better if you exercise. It keeps you fit. Exercise makes your body stronger. It can also help you to relax. If you are worried or angry about something, exercise can help you feel better. Consider the following situation, for example.

Yesterday, Robert had a bad day at the food store where he works. By 5:00, he was very upset. Usually Robert goes home and watches TV all night when he is upset. But he feels even worse when he does that. This time, Robert changed into sweat pants and a T-shirt when he got home. Then he went to a gym. He worked out for half an hour doing exercises. Then he took a long, slow swim.

When he got home again, Robert felt much better. The problem at work was not **solved**, or taken care of. But, now Robert was relaxed. He had worked out some of his **frustration**. He was not so **stressed**, or tense. Even his problems at work did not seem as upsetting.

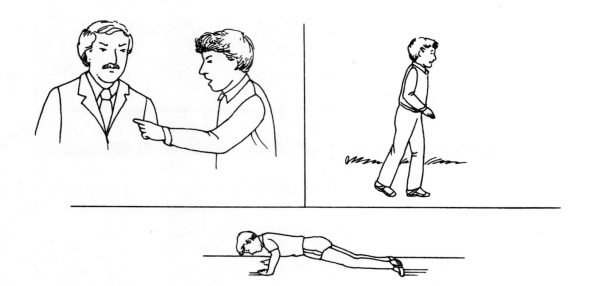

Exercise is important. Studies show that people who exercise every day are healthier. They have fewer problems with their hearts and their **circulation**—the flow of blood through the body. Their lungs are stronger, too. In general, they feel better. And some people find that they eat less and smoke less if they exercise regularly.

You can **increase**, or make greater, how much you exercise in simple ways. If you drive a lot, don't park right next to where you are going. Instead, park at the end of the parking lot and walk. If you take a bus and walk to the bus stop, increase your walking speed. This will get your heart going a little faster. In buildings, try to use stairs instead of elevators. At home, do some simple exercises when you wake up or before meals.

There are many places where you can exercise:

- a school ball field

- the local YMCA or YWCA (Young Men's or Young Women's Christian Associations)

- a gym

- a boxing club

- the town swimming pool

- your living room floor

Some people like to exercise alone. Others find it is easier to exercise with a friend. Many people enjoy exercising with one of their kids. However you decide to do it, exercise is good for you. Exercise helps you relax. It improves your circulation. It helps you sleep better. Exercising can even help you lose weight. You can burn 200–300 calories in an hour just by walking.

Exercise helps you relax and keeps your body fit. Try to exercise every day. Start slowly. Increase the amount you exercise over several weeks. This way, exercising will be easier. It will also be more fun.

REVIEW

Choose the best answer. Circle it. Go back to the reading to check your answers. The first one is done for you.

1. Robert went to the gym because he _____.
    a. was alone at home
    (b.) was upset and frustrated
    c. missed a TV show

2. After exercising, Robert _____.
    a. solved the problem
    b. was too angry
    c. was less stressed

3. People who exercise regularly _____.
    a. have more problems
    b. have better circulation
    c. are upset

4. One way to get more exercise is to _____.
    a. use the stairs
    b. use the elevator
    c. drive a lot

5. Just by walking for an hour, you can burn _____.
    a. 500 calories
    b. 200–300 calories
    c. 1 calorie

6. The main idea of this reading is _____.
    a. exercise is good for us
    b. where to exercise
    c. do not exercise too much at first

PRACTICE

A. Choose a word. Complete each sentence with a word or phrase from the list below. Write the answer in the space. The first one is done for you.

          burns off   **circulation**   **increase**
          solve   **stressed**

1. Robert needed to **solve** his problem at work.

2. Our _____ is better if we exercise regularly.

3. Walking _____ about 300 calories an hour.

4. It is good to start slowly and then _____ the amount of exercise.

5. Robert felt less _____after exercising.

B. Choose a time to exercise. Exercising can be enjoyable. But when can you exercise? Check the times when you could exercise. An example is done for you.

    √   1. at 6:00 a.m.

             2. half an hour before breakfast

             3. during part of my lunch hour

             4. when I get home from work

             5. before dinner

             6. every weekend

             7. other _____

C. What can you say? A friend makes each of the statements below. What would you say to your friend? Write your ideas on the blank lines. The first one is done for you.

1. I would like to exercise more. What can I do?

   __Try using the stairs instead of the elevator.__

   _____

2. It is hard for me to relax these days.

   _____

   _____

3. Why should I walk to work? It is a lot easier to drive my car.

   _____

   _____

4. I want to try swimming for exercise. How should I start?

   _____

   _____

D. Which way to go? You decide to walk for exercise. Where will you walk? Write down your ideas on routes near your home that you can take. One example is given for you.

1. __Walk down 2nd St., around the park, and back.__

2. _____

3. _____

4. _____

UNIT 18

Where Does the Time Go?

This unit is about:

- managing your time

Think About

What do you do every day?
What things do you have to do? What things do you like to
   do?
Do you feel you have enough time each day to get things
   done?

Where Does the Time Go?

Kevin was starting a new job. He set his alarm clock. The next morning he got up. By the time he did everything he needed to do, he had to **rush** to get to work on time. He thought he had set his alarm clock early enough, but he had not. He felt stressed by the time he got to work. It was not a good way to start a new job.

Starting something new changes our lives. A new job or a new school changes our schedules. We may no longer have enough time for some things we used to do. But some things—such as having meals and getting dressed— *have* to get done. How can we organize our time?

Make a list. Write down the things you *must* get done, such as getting dressed. Write down how long it takes you to do each thing. Maybe it takes you 15 minutes to get dressed; 5 minutes to wash your face and comb your hair. Then, write down the things that you like to do, but that are not really necessary. For example, you might like to sit quietly and drink a cup of coffee in the morning. It is not absolutely necessary. But, that cup of coffee makes you feel better about starting the day.

Look at Kevin's list below:

Take a shower and shave	15 minutes
Get dressed	10 minutes
Have breakfast	20 minutes
Make lunch	10 minutes
Get son ready for day care	20 minutes
Take son to **day-care center**	20 minutes
Drive to work	25 minutes
Total	120 minutes = 2 hours

Kevin made his list. He **discovered** that he needed two hours between waking up and getting to work. The first morning he only gave himself one and one-half hours. Kevin needs to either:

- Get up earlier.

  OR

- Change his routine.

What can he do differently? He can decide to make his lunch the night before. He can also prepare his son's bag for day care at night. This will save him time in the morning.

Managing time is not always easy. There are many things we need to do every day. A new job gives us less free time. We have to be organized. Making a list can help us. The list reminds us of what we need to do. And, it tells us how much time we need. It can help us start something more easily.

REVIEW

Choose the best answer. Circle it. Go back to the reading to check your answers. The first one is done for you.

1. Kevin felt _____ by the time he got to work.
   a. happy
   (b.) stressed
   c. tired

2. A new job may give us _____.
   a. less free time
   b. more free time
   c. less to do

3. _____ can help us get organized.
   a. Making a list
   b. Going to work
   c. Using an alarm clock

4. Something *necessary* is something we _____ do.
   a. can
   b. must
   c. like to

5. Kevin can save time in the morning by _____.
   a. eating his breakfast
   b. taking a shower
   c. making lunch at night

6. Another title for this reading could be _____.
   a. Working
   b. How to Get Organized
   c. Waking Up on Time

PRACTICE

A. What is your day like? What is a regular day for you? Below list all of the things you usually do. Include what you have to do and what you like to do. One idea is given for you.

Take my dog for a walk.

_____

_____

_____

_____

_____

_____

_____

_____

_____

B. What is most important? In what order would you put the things you usually do? What do you think is most important? What do you think is least important? Put **1** next to what is most important. Put **2** next to what is second. Write the numbers on the lines above in Exercise **A**.

C. Whoops! Schedule change. Imagine you start a new job. The job is from 3 p.m. to 11 p.m. How would this change the schedule you have now? Write your ideas on the lines below. One idea is given for you.

   I would not eat dinner with my family.

_____

_____

_____

_____

_____

D. Describe a free day. You have a free day. You can do whatever you want. What would you do? Describe your day on the lines below. One suggestion is given for you.

   First, I would stay in bed until 10:00 a.m.

_____

_____

_____

_____

UNIT 19

Fill In the Blanks

This unit is about:

- filling out forms

- words you find on forms

Think About

When was the last time you had to fill out a form? What questions were asked?
Was it easy or difficult to fill out?

Fill In the Blanks

Today, we are often asked to fill out a form: to get a job, to open a bank account, to see a dentist, or to get a car loan.

Most forms have a part that asks for personal data. *Data* is simply another word for *information*. So *personal data* means information about you and your personal life. Read the form below and then try filling it out:

PERSONAL DATA

Name _____
         (Last)   (First)   (Middle)

Address _____
        (No. & Street)

_____
    (City)   (State)   (Zip)

Permanent
address _____
      (No. & Street)

_____
    (City)   (State)   (Zip)

Phone no. _____ Social Security no. _____

Date of birth _____ Age _____

Height _____ Weight _____

Marital status _____

No. of dependents _____

On this form, *No.* and *no.* are used as abbreviations for *number*. On some other forms # is the abbreviation for number. A **Social Security number** is your personal number. It always has a total of nine numbers. You need such a number to get a job or open a bank account. You can get a Social Security number easily. Just call the Social Security office in your area.

Some forms may ask you for a permanent address—a place you can always be reached. If you do not move often, write *same as above* on this blank. If you move a lot, you can use a relative's address.

Some of the words on the form may be new. What did you write for **marital status**? There are several possible answers to this question: single, married, divorced, separated, or widowed. *Separated* means that you are not living with your **spouse**—your husband or wife—but you are not divorced. *Widowed* means that your spouse has died.

What about *no. of **dependents***? Your dependents are family members who (1) live with you and (2) depend on you for food and housing. A non-working spouse and your children are your dependents. If you have three children and a spouse at home, you have four dependents. An older parent you **support** is also a dependent.

Here are a few suggestions to make filling out forms easier:

- Read over the form carefully before filling it in.
- Always give correct information. If something is confusing, ask for help. Don't just make a guess.
- Keep the form neat. Avoid scratching out answers. If you make several mistakes, ask for a new form. A messy form gives a bad **impression**—the way you look to other people.

Filling out forms is not always easy. Most people have questions when they fill out forms. Always ask for help if there is something you do not understand.

REVIEW

Choose the best answer. Circle it. Go back to the reading to check your answers. The first one is done for you.

1. The abbreviation *no.* means _____.
    a. none
    b. no one
    c. number

2. If you don't move often, write _____ for your permanent address.
    a. a relative's address
    b. your Social Security number
    c. same as above

3. To open a bank account you need _____.
    a. dependents
    b. a Social Security number
    c. a relative's address

4. A spouse is _____.
    a. a husband or wife
    b. only a husband
    c. only a wife

5. Young children who live at home are called _____.
    a. permanent
    b. dependents
    c. spouses

6. If you don't know how to answer something on a form, _____.
    a. write anything
    b. leave it blank
    c. find out

PRACTICE

A. Filling out forms. Read the paragraph below. Use the information in the paragraph to fill out the form. Look back at the reading if you need help.

Judith Ann Henry is looking for a job as a hostess at a small restaurant in her neighborhood. She lives at 15 Stuart Avenue in Detroit, Michigan. The zip code is 48201. She has lived there for ten years. Judith was born on July 16, 1962 in Chicago, Illinois. Her home telephone number is (313) 555-5423. She does not have a job yet so she has no work phone. Her Social Security number is 111-67-9145. Judith has two children. Her children's names are Robert and Martin. Her husband died in 1988.

PERSONAL DATA (Please print)			
Name	(Last)	(First)	(Middle)
Address	(No. & Street)		
	(City)	(State)	(Zip)
Permanent address	(No. & Street)		
	(City)	(State)	(Zip)
Home phone: ( ) Work phone: ( )		Social Security no. — —	
Date of birth / /	Age	Place of birth	
Marital status ☐ Single ☐ Married ☐ Divorced ☐ Separated ☐ Widowed			
Spouse's name	(Last)	(First)	(Middle)
Spouse's date of birth / /	Age	Place of birth	
Other dependents	Dependents' names		

B. What would you say? Each person below is filling out a form. They ask you for some help. What would you say to them? Write your answers on the lines below. The first one is done for you.

1. Eddie is filling out a form to apply for a job. He has made a lot of mistakes. He crossed them out.

   __He should ask for a new form.__

   _____

2. Luisa's husband died a short time ago. She is filling out a form at the bank. Luisa is not sure what *marital status* means. She does not know which box to mark.

   _____

   _____

3. Suki works in a hotel kitchen. She is divorced and has three children. Her 70-year-old mother lives with them and is ill. Suki does not know what to write for *no. of dependents*.

   _____

   _____

4. Jill is renting a room while she looks for an apartment. She wants to get training to be a cook's assistant. The form she must fill out at a night school asks for a permanent address.

   _____

   _____

5. Al has been married two years. He is filling out a form at the supermarket. He wants to be able to cash checks there. What should he write on the line asking *spouse's name?*

   _____

   _____

UNIT **20**

What Are You Good At?

This unit is about:

- finding what you are good at

- finding what you like to do

Think About

What things are you good at?
What things do you like to do?

What Are You Good At?

What do you like doing? What are you good at? Thinking about your interests and **abilities** can help you find the right **career**, or job, in a food service.

Everybody is able to do something well. Some people can fix things. Some people can cook well. Others are good at talking with people. Everybody has some special ability. In fact, you are probably good at more than one thing. Look at the list of abilities below. Which of the following are you good at?

TYPES OF ABILITIES
1. Working with numbers
2. Making people feel at ease
3. Art
4. Working with your hands
5. Cooking
6. Working quickly and accurately with lists
7. Working with machines

Now, think for a minute about your interests. Do you enjoy working with people? If so, you might like a job in a restaurant as a host or hostess. Are you artistic? That is, are you good at art? You might like arranging food on plates or decorating cakes.

Maybe you prefer working with numbers and other written records. You might like working in a food-service office ordering food. Do you like keeping track of things? Are you well-organized? Then, you might like being in charge of a food-service storeroom ordering and weighing foods.

Perhaps you have **mechanical** interests—you like working with machines. If so, you might like a job working with large cooking or baking machines.

Of course, you probably have more than one interest. Maybe you like working with both people and food. If so, you might enjoy working as a **waitperson**. On the other hand, if you don't like working with a lot of people, you might be happier in the kitchen. You could work as a cook or as an assistant, helping the cook.

There are special tests to help you find your interests and abilities. A counselor at your neighborhood center or school can help you. After you find what your interests and abilities are, you can think about jobs that **suit** you best. You will probably be surprised—there are many different jobs that match your special interests and abilities.

REVIEW

Choose the best answer. Circle it. Go back to the reading to check your answers. The first one is done for you.

1. Which of the following is true about abilities?
   a. Some people aren't good at anything.
   (b.) Everybody is good at something.
   c. Everybody is good at everything.

2. Another way to say *keep track of things* is _____.
   a. be organized
   b. get going
   c. work with numbers

3. Alberto decorates cakes and makes special pies. Which type of ability does he probably have?
   a. working with numbers
   b. artistic ability
   c. understanding mechanical things

4. A person who enjoys working with people and food might like a job as a _____.
   a. counselor
   b. waitress
   c. cashier

5. A _____ can help you identify the jobs that suit you best.
   a. counselor
   b. bookkeeper
   c. cashier

6. Another title for this reading could be _____.
   a. Finding the Right Job
   b. Working with Your Hands
   c. Helping Other People

PRACTICE

A. Where could they fit in? Below are descriptions of people who are thinking of a career in food service. Where do you think they could fit in? Write all the jobs you can think of for each person. They do not have to be from the reading. The first one is done for you.

1. Joyce is good with numbers and is very friendly to people.

   She could be a cashier in a restaurant. Or she

   could be a waitress.

   _____

2. Simon is shy and artistic. He would like to use his artistic ability in a food-service job.

   _____

   _____

   _____

3. Gena loves children. She would like to have a food-service job where she can be with children.

   _____

   _____

   _____

4. Louis grew up on a farm and loves to cook and bake at home.

   _____

   _____

   _____

B. Is this the right job? Read the want ad below. Think about the abilities and interests needed for this job. Read the questions. Put a check mark under the correct answer. The first one is done for you.

Assistant Cook
Large restaurant needs assistant cook who can work well under pressure. Responsible for preparing salads and vegetable dishes. Some weekend work required. One–two years' experience needed. Come to 10 Main St. for an interview and ask for Rita or Charles. No calls please.

	YES	NO
1. Is this a good job for someone who can handle pressure?	√	
2. Would you probably need to cut vegetables for this job?		
3. Should you apply for this job if you have no experience?		
4. Do they want people to call before coming in for an interview?		
5. Would a person who can work on weekends be right for this job?		
6. Do you think you would do well in this job?		

ANSWER KEYS

Keep It Balanced   UNIT 1

REVIEW

1. c   3. a   5. b
2. a   4. a   6. c

PRACTICE

A. Where do these foods belong?

apples   corn flakes   fish
milk   peanuts   potatoes

Fruits and Vegetables	Dairy Foods	Breads and Cereals	Meats
apples *potatoes*	milk	*corn flakes*	*fish* *peanuts*

B. Which food is from a different food group?

1. chicken   <u>cheese</u>   pork chops   fish
2. bananas   carrots   lemons   <u>yogurt</u>
3. milk   yogurt   <u>cereal</u>   ice cream
4. <u>steak</u>   bread   rolls   crackers
5. grapes   <u>nuts</u>   tomatoes   oranges
6. <u>tomatoes</u>   yogurt   cheese   milk

C. What did you eat yesterday? *(More than one answer is possible. Check with your instructor or tutor.)*

1. Did you have food from all four food groups?

   _____

2. If not, which food group is missing from your list?

   _____

D. Keep a record of what you eat. *(More than one answer is possible. Check with your instructor or tutor.)*

Food Group	Day 1	Day 2
Fruits and Vegetables	orange juice	
Dairy Foods		
Breads and Cereals	toast	
Meats		

REVIEW

1. c	3. a	5. c
2. b	4. b	6. a

PRACTICE

A. Think about your eating habits. *(More than one answer is possible. Check with your instructor or tutor.)*

	Often	Some- times	Never
1. Do you eat at regular times?			
2. Do you snack?			
3. Do you eat sweet snacks?			
4. Does the weather affect what you eat?			
5. Do you drink lots of water every day?			
6. Do you eat balanced meals?			
7. Do you watch TV during mealtimes?			
8. Do you eat while you work?			
9. Do you sit down at the table to eat?			
10. Do you eat with your family?			

B. What do you suggest? *(More than one answer is possible. Check with your instructor or tutor.)*

1. A friend's son loves to snack. He eats potato chips and cookies as he watches TV after school. Then, he is not hungry at dinner.

    __Your friend should make sure fruits and vegetables are__

    __around to snack on and hide the chips and cookies.__

    _____

2. Your boss always eats a donut in the car on her way to work. Later, she complains that her stomach hurts her.

    __Your boss should not eat on the run. She should take__

    __the time to eat a good breakfast at home.__

    _____

3. In the summer Carlos works outside all day. He drinks lots of coffee for breakfast and lunch. He still feels very thirsty.

    __He should drink cold water or fruit juice.__

    _____

    _____

4. Will is very busy. Sometimes he eats just one meal a day. When he eats, he usually has a hamburger and fries.

    __He should eat a balanced meal at least twice a day.__

    _____

    _____

Get Out That List!

REVIEW

1. b   3. b   5. c

2. c   4. a   6. b

PRACTICE

A. Choose a word.

cookies	**coupons**	**food ads**
macaroni & cheese		**refrigerator**

1. It is a good idea to check the __**food ads**__ before you shop.

2. Cutting out __*coupons*__ can help you save money.

3. A good place to keep a list is on the __*refrigerator*__ .

4. __*Cookies*__ are a kind of treat.

5. An example of a packaged food is __*macaroni & cheese*__ .

B. Make a shopping list. (*More than one answer is possible. Check with your instructor or tutor.*)

__a dozen eggs__

_____

_____

_____

_____

C. Think about your shopping habits. *(More than one answer is possible. Check with your instructor or tutor.)*

	Often	Some-times	Never
1. Do you make a shopping list?			
2. If you make a list, do you stick to it?			
3. Do you check the newspaper for specials?			
4. Do you try to use coupons?			
5. Do you go shopping on an empty stomach?			
6. Do you buy something because you like the box?			
7. Do you read labels?			
8. Do you check your cart before you go to the checkout?			

D. What do you suggest? *(More than one answer is possible. Check with your instructor or tutor.)*

<u>use coupons</u>

_____

_____

What's in It?

REVIEW

1. b	3. c	5. a
2. a	4. b	6. b

PRACTICE

A. Which would you buy?

> **Baby Food A: Baby's Chicken Dinner**
> ingredients: water, carrots, chicken, potatoes, peas, rice flour, corn, dry milk, wheat flour, oil, flavorings

> **Baby Food B: Baby's Yummy Chicken Surprise**
> ingredients: water, potatoes, rice flour, potato starch, carrots, peas, corn, chicken, dry milk, wheat flour, oil, flavorings

	Baby Food A	Baby Food B
1. Which ingredient is rice flour?	**6th**	**3rd**
2. Which ingredient is chicken?	*3rd*	*8th*
3. Which ingredient is carrots?	*2nd*	*5th*
4. Which ingredient is potatoes?	*4th*	*2nd*

5. Which baby food seems better? Why? _Baby Food A because_

   it has more chicken and vegetables and less starch.

B. Label detective at home. *(More than one answer is possible. Check with your instructor or tutor.)*

1. __Crackers: wheat flour, shortening, salt, yeast,__ __sugar__

2. _____

   _____

3. _____

   _____

4. _____

   _____

5. _____

   _____

6. _____

   _____

REVIEW

1. a   3. c   5. b
2. b   4. a   6. a

PRACTICE

A. Choose the correct word.

choices	economical	good
picks up	store brand	tastes

1. It is important to try to be __**economical**__ when we shop.

2. The _store brand_ is often cheaper.

3. There are a lot of _choices_ at the grocery store.

4. Marie _picks up_ some TV dinners.

5. Marie wants something that _tastes_ good.

6. Marie also wants something that is _good_ for her family.

B. List some quick foods. *(More than one answer is possible. Check with your instructor or tutor.)*

Name	Ingredients
canned stew	meat, potatoes, carrots, onions, water

C. What would you buy? *(More than one answer is possible. Check with your instructor or tutor.)*

1. __Frozen cheese pizza. It is made with cheese,__ __tomatoes, and bread dough.__

2. *__Frozen fish sticks, macaroni and cheese, frozen__* *__vegetables.__*

3. *__Packaged salad with meat from the deli.__*

_____

4. _____

_____

5. _____

_____

6. _____

_____

REVIEW

1. b	3. c	5. a
2. a	4. c	6. c

PRACTICE

A. What would you say? *(More than one answer is possible. Check with your instructor or tutor.)*

1. Thomas wakes up late. He cuts his hand making breakfast. He runs into work, takes off his jacket, and starts cutting up vegetables right away.

   <u>**He should wash his hands and wear gloves.**</u>

   _____

2. Ann is in a hurry. She takes a chicken from her grocery bag and throws it right into a pot on the stove.

   <u>*She should rinse the chicken off first.*</u>

   _____

3. Theresa spills some sugar. She leaves it on the counter.

   <u>*She should wipe it up right away.*</u>

   _____

4. Carl uses the same knife to cut up meat and then the salad vegetables.

   <u>*He should wash the knife before cutting the vegetables.*</u>

   _____

B. Vocabulary practice.

contamination	gloves	handling
rinsing	soapy	utensil

1. Using two cutting boards reduces __contamination__ .

2. Use hot, _soapy_ water to wash your hands.

3. Wash your hands after _handling_ uncooked chicken.

4. Wear _gloves_ if you have a cut.

5. _Rinsing_ chicken helps remove germs.

6. A knife is a kitchen _utensil_ .

C. What would you do?

1. Wash your hands with hot, soapy water.   _1_

2. Cut the chicken on a cutting board.   _3_

3. Finally, wash your hands again.   _5_

4. Wash the cutting board with soap and water.   _4_

5. Rinse the chicken carefully.   _2_

REVIEW

1. c   3. a   5. b
2. a   4. c   6. b

PRACTICE

A. What is wrong with this kitchen?

1. ___There is a carton of milk on the counter.___

2. ___There is a chicken on the counter.___

3. ___There are fresh vegetables left on the counter.___

4. ___There is some cooked food left on the stove.___

5. ___The food in the refrigerator is not covered.___

B. What do you suggest? *(More than one answer is possible. Check with your instructor or tutor.)*

Keep the counter clean.

_____

_____

_____

C. Do or don't?

Do	Don't	
	√	Eat spoiled food.
	√	Eat strange-smelling food.
√		Throw away food that looks strange.
√		Put food in the refrigerator.
	√	Leave cooked food out overnight.
√		Use clean storage containers.
√		Cover food well.
	√	Store leftovers a long time.

A Cold? No, Thanks!   UNIT **8**

REVIEW

1. b   3. b   5. a

2. a   4. a   6. c

PRACTICE

A. Yes or no?

1. You have a cold. What should you do?

	YES	NO
cover your mouth when you sneeze	√	
visit friends		√
rest	√	
stay up late		√

2. You want to avoid getting a cold.
    What should you do?

	YES	NO
visit friends who are sick		√
keep your hands near your mouth		√
get plenty of rest	√	
eat right	√	
avoid washing your hands		√

B. What do you do? *(More than one answer is possible. Check with your instructor or tutor.)*

__Drink lots of tea with honey and lemon.__

Stay inside for the first 24 hours.

C. Go to work or stay home? *(More than one answer is possible. Check with your instructor or tutor.)*

1. a cook   _A cook has to touch other people's food._
   A cook should probably stay home.

   _____

2. a carpenter   _A carpenter doesn't work that closely with_
   people. He would probably go to work.

   _____

3. a teacher   _Teachers should not go to work if they have a_
   cold. Their germs may spread.

   _____

4. a police officer   _He could go to work if he doesn't work directly_
   with other people.

   _____

5. a waiter or waitress   _They have too much contact with food and the_
   public. They should probably stay home.

   _____

6. a meat cutter   _A meat cutter has too much contact with food. He_
   or she should stay home.

   _____

A Healthy Mouth

REVIEW

1. a   3. b   5. a
2. b   4. c   6. b

PRACTICE

A. Do or don't?

Do	Don't	
√		Brush your teeth after every meal.
	√	Eat a lot of candy and sugar.
	√	Let a baby fall asleep with a bottle.
√		Floss your teeth every day.
	√	Avoid going to the dentist.
	√	Wait until a problem gets big.
√		Have the hygienist clean your teeth.
√		Go to the dentist regularly.

B. Choose a word.

avoid	booklet	checked
habit	hurt	meal

1. The dentist __checked__ Angela's teeth.

2. Angela read the _booklet_ on her way home.

3. Try to _avoid_ sweet foods.

4. Brush after every _meal_ .

5. Some people think dentists will _hurt_ them.

6. Flossing every day is a good _habit_ .

C. Write some rules. *(More than one answer is possible. Check with your instructor or tutor.)*

	Rules for a Healthy Mouth
Cavities	**Brush and floss teeth so you won't get cavities.**
Sweet foods	*Avoid sweet foods.*
Baby bottles	*Don't let a baby sleep with a bottle.*
Water	*Drink some water if you cannot brush.*
Brush	*Brush after every meal.*
Floss	*Floss once a day.*
Dentist	*Go to the dentist regularly.*

Kitchen Safety

REVIEW

1. c   3. a   5. c

2. b   4. b   6. b

PRACTICE

A. Kitchen safety. *(More than one answer is possible. Check with your instructor or tutor.)*

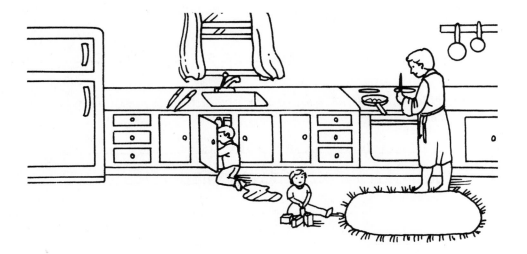

1. __Turn the handle of the pan inward.__

2. *Wipe up the spill.*

3. *Lock the cabinet.*

4. *Put knives out of children's reach.*

5. *Keep curtains away from the stove.*

B.   Why is it dangerous? *(More than one answer is possible. Check with your instructor or tutor.)*

1. Singu left some soup cooking while he ran to the post office.

    __A fire could start._____

2. Maria often leaves the handles of her pots sticking out.

    __*A child could knock the pots over.*_____

3. Thomas keeps sharp knives in the same drawer as his forks and spoons.

    __*He could grab a knife by accident and cut himself.*_____

4. Margo puts bleach in soda bottles because it is easier to pour.

    __*Someone might think it is soda and drink it.*_____

5. Alex uses an extension cord for his coffee pot. He likes to keep it on the kitchen table.

    __*Someone could easily trip over the cord and spill the coffee.*__

C.   Take a look around. *(More than one answer is possible. Check with your instructor or tutor.)*

1. __Put child locks on my cabinets._____

2. __*Plug up electrical sockets with plastic plug covers.*_____

3. _____

4. _____

5. _____

REVIEW

1. b	3. a	5. a
2. c	4. c	6. b

PRACTICE

A. Do or don't?

D o	Don't	
	√	Leave matches on the stove.
√		Wipe up grease on the stove.
√		Pay attention to the clothes you wear.
√		Watch hot oil carefully.
	√	Hang curtains near the stove.
	√	Disconnect the smoke detector.
√		Always have some baking soda.
	√	Use a charcoal grill indoors.

B. Say it another way.

1. Theresa *put on* her robe.

   __Theresa threw on her robe.__

2. Theresa was *cooking* some fried eggs.

   Theresa was fixing some fried eggs.

3. She *put* her arm under the cold water.

   She stuck her arm under the cold water.

4. Theresa was *frightened.*

   Theresa was scared.

5. The chart was about *keeping fires from happening*.

   The chart was about fire prevention.

6. Nylon is a *man-made* material.

   Nylon is a synthetic material.

C. What would you suggest? *(More than one answer is possible. Check with your instructor or tutor.)*

1. Walter always leaves his stove covered with grease.

   He should clean it. It is not safe.

2. Sonja usually wears a loose robe when she cooks breakfast.

   She should change clothes. Her sleeve might catch fire.

3. Vim keeps his matches in a box on the stove.

   He should move them away from the heat.

4. Kim just bought long nylon curtains for the window above his stove.

   He shouldn't use them. They might catch on fire.

5. Horacio took the battery out of his smoke detector. He doesn't like the sound it makes when the battery is low.

   He should put a new one in right away.

REVIEW

1. c   3. b   5. b
2. b   4. c   6. a

PRACTICE

A. Choose the correct word.

clean   elevate   first aid
pressure   water

1. Give __first aid__ right after someone is hurt.

2. Put cold _water_ on a simple burn.

3. _Clean_ a cut, then put on a bandage.

4. Sometimes you can stop the bleeding by applying _____

   pressure .

5. If you _elevate_, or raise, a cut the bleeding may slow down.

B. What would you suggest? *(More than one answer is possible. Check with your instructor or tutor.)*

1. Dori got a small cut on her finger.

   __I would wash the cut and put a bandage on it.__

2. Jose spilled boiling soup on his arm.

   Put his arm under cold water until the pain stops.

3. Vim cut his thumb. It is bleeding a lot.

   Elevate his hand and apply pressure to his thumb.

4. Teddie cut himself. He is scared.

   Help him to stay calm. Give him first aid.

C. Read about the first-aid courses.

South End Hospital
14 Broadway, Rockaway, NY

325-2550

We are pleased to offer free first-aid classes. Below is a description of each with the days and times. If you are interested in taking any of them, please call Special Services at 325-2550. We look forward to seeing you.

First Aid for Beginners:
Learn about common emergencies (cuts, burns, broken bones). Monday & Wednesday 6:30-9:00pm.

Advanced First Aid:
Learn about head injuries, choking, heart attacks, and bandaging. Tuesday & Thursday 6:30-9:00pm.

Water Safety:
Learn about problems and emergencies that happen near the water - how to prevent and handle them. Wednesday 6:00-9:00pm.

Child Safety:
Learn what problems and situations are common for children. Monday 7:00-9:30pm.

---

1. Where are the courses taught? _at South End Hospital_

2. How much do the courses cost? _They are free._

3. If you have not taken a first-aid course before, which one would be good

   to take first? _First Aid for Beginners_

4. Which course teaches you about water emergencies?

   Water Safety

5. Which course meets on Monday night? _Child Safety_

6. Which course teaches about head injuries? _Advanced_

   First Aid

For Cooking, Not Heating   UNIT **13**

REVIEW

1. c   3. a   5. b

2. b   4. c   6. b

PRACTICE

A. Choose a word.

carbon monoxide	dangerous	
gas company	recognize	spark

1. Heating with a kitchen stove is __dangerous__ .

2. Leaking gas is easy to _recognize_ .

3. Call the _gas company_ for help.

4. _Carbon monoxide_ can build up if we use a gas oven for heating.

5. The telephone can release a _spark_ .

B. What should you do first?

1. Open the doors and windows.   _4_

2. Check the pilot light.   _2_

3. Call the gas company.   _6_

4. You smell some gas.   _1_

5. The pilot light is O.K.   _3_

6. Go to a neighbor's house or pay phone.   _5_

C. What do you suggest? *(More than one answer is possible. Check with your instructor or tutor.)*

Close the curtains at night.

_____

_____

_____

_____

_____

D. Know those numbers. *(More than one answer is possible. Check with your instructor or tutor.)*

1. Look up the telephone numbers of the utility companies in your area.

2. Check the front of the phone book to see if there is a number in your area to call for help with heating. Try looking under *Heating Assistance.* What is the number?

Utility	Number
electricity	
gas	
sewer	
telephone	
water	

Getting Help When You Need It

REVIEW

1. b   3. a   5. a

2. c   4. c   6. b

PRACTICE

A. Did she say the right thing?

911:	Emergency. What's the matter?
Mari:	We need help. There's been an accident!
911:	OK. I need your name.
Mari:	Mari Sihng. S-I-H-N-G. My sister fell. Her head is bleeding a lot.
911:	Where are you?
Mari:	In the kitchen.
911:	Is your sister conscious? Is she awake?
Mari:	Yes, but she's bleeding very bad. Please send someone. I have to help her now. Good-bye.

1. Did Mari give her name?   <u>YES</u>   NO
2. Did she give the address?   YES   <u>NO</u>
3. Did she say what the problem was?   <u>YES</u>   NO
4. Did she say what help she needed?   <u>YES</u>   NO

B. What should he say?

Stuart Low lives with his family at 231 Kennedy Street, in a second floor apartment. His grandfather has just slipped and fallen in the kitchen. He is holding his hip and groaning. He says he thinks he broke something. He says the pain is terrible. Stuart is afraid to move him for fear of hurting him more. He calls 911.

<u>My name is Stuart Low. I am at 231 Kennedy St., second floor. My grandfather has just slipped and fallen. He is holding his hip and groaning. He says he thinks he broke something. I'm afraid to move him, so please send an ambulance.</u>

C. Choose the correct word.

accident   ambulance   emergency room
EMT   operator

1. A man at the restaurant was in an __accident__ .

2. We need an __ambulance__ to get him to the hospital.

3. I called the __operator__ for emergency help.

4. The __EMT__ gave the man first aid.

5. At the __emergency room__ a nurse helped him.

D. List your emergency numbers. *(More than one answer is possible. Check with your instructor or tutor.)*

Name	Telephone Number
Emergency	911
Doctor	
Ambulance	
Police	
Fire Department	
Hospital	
Parents' work numbers	

148

REVIEW

1. b	3. a	5. b
2. c	4. c	6. b

PRACTICE

A. Choose a word.

2 Tbl.	**abbreviations**	**accurately**
cup	**equivalent**	**tablespoon**

1. A __cup__ is a unit of measurement.

2. It is important to measure _accurately_ .

3. _Abbreviations_ are often used in directions on packages.

4. Two measurements that are _equivalent_ are the same.

5. One ounce is the same as _2 Tbl._ .

6. A _tablespoon_ is bigger than a teaspoon.

B. What does it stand for?

1. __three cups of flour__	3 c. flour
2. _two pints of juice_	2 pt. juice
3. _four ounces of water_	4 oz. water
4. _two quarts of milk_	2 qt. milk
5. _one tablespoon of oil_	1 Tbl. oil
6. _two teaspoons of salt_	2 tsp. salt
7. _three tablespoons of sugar_	3 tbsp. sugar
8. _three gallons of honey_	3 gal. honey

C. What is it the same as?

1. __1 gallon of milk__   4 qt. milk

2. _1 cup of oil_   16 Tbl. oil

3. _four tablespoons of butter_   1/4 c. butter

4. _one tablespoon of salt_   3 tsp. salt

5. _1 pint or 16 ounces of milk_   2 c. milk

6. _2 pints or 1 quart of juice_   4 c. juice

D. At the grocery store. *(More than one answer is possible. Check with your instructor or tutor.)*

A Name of product	B Contents
1. __corn flakes__	__9 oz. (nine ounces)__
2.	
3.	
4.	
5.	
6.	

More or Less

REVIEW

1. b   3. c   5. b

2. a   4. b   6. a

PRACTICE

A. What difference does it make?

FOOD and CALORIES	
1 medium potato, baked	90
1 serving mashed potatoes with milk	125
1 serving french fries	250
1 serving corn flakes, plain	100
1 serving corn flakes, sugar-coated	155
1 serving canned peaches, heavy syrup	90
1 serving canned peaches, light syrup	38
1 fresh peach	35
1 slice of toast, plain	60
butter for toast	35
strawberry jam for toast	55
1 chicken breast, no skin, baked	115
1 chicken breast, fried	155
1 serving canned corn, regular kernel	70
1 serving canned corn, cream style	100

1. How many calories does a serving of plain corn flakes have?

   __**100 calories**__

2. How many more calories does a serving of sugar-coated corn flakes

   have? _55 more calories_

151

3. If you want a potato for dinner, which kind has the most calories? _french fries_

4. Compare the canned peaches. How many *more* calories do peaches in heavy syrup have? _90 – 38 = 52_

5. Which type of chicken breast has 155 calories?

   the fried chicken breast

6. Look at the corn. Which has more calories, cream-style or regular kernel? _cream-style_

7. How many calories does a slice of plain toast have?

   _60_

8. How many calories are in a slice of toast with butter and jam?

   _150_

B. You decide. *(More than one answer is possible. Check with your instructor or tutor.)*

   I could eat fewer french fries.

   _____

   _____

   _____

   _____

   _____

   _____

REVIEW

1. b	3. b	5. b
2. c	4. a	6. a

PRACTICE

A. Choose a word. Complete each sentence with a word or phrase from the list below. Write the answer in the space. The first one is done for you.

> burns off   circulation   increase
> solve   stressed

1. Robert needed to ___solve_____ his problem at work.

2. Our _circulation_____ is better if we exercise regularly.

3. Walking _burns off_____ about 300 calories an hour.

4. It is good to start slowly and then _increase_____ the amount of exercise.

5. Robert felt less _stressed_____after exercising.

B. Choose a time to exercise. Exercising can be enjoyable. But when can you exercise? Check the times when you could exercise. An example is done for you.

___√____   1. at 6:00 a.m.

_____   2. half an hour before breakfast

_____   3. during part of my lunch hour

_____   4. when I get home from work

_____   5. before dinner

_____   6. every weekend

_____   7. other _____

C. What can you say? *(More than one answer is possible. Check with your instructor or tutor.)*

1. I would like to exercise more. What can I do?

   <u>Try using the stairs instead of the elevator.</u>

   _____

2. It is hard for me to relax these days.

   <u>Maybe you need to work off some of your energy.</u>

   <u>Think about going to the town swimming pool.</u>

3. Why should I walk to work? It is a lot easier to drive my car.

   <u>Walking is really good exercise. And exercise can make</u>

   <u>you feel a lot better.</u>

4. I want to try swimming for exercise. How should I start?

   <u>Call the local YMCA or YWCA. They sometimes have</u>

   <u>swimming classes.</u>

D. Which way to go? *(More than one answer is possible. Check with your instructor or tutor.)*

1. <u>**Walk down 2nd St., around the park, and back.**</u>

2. _____

3. _____

4. _____

154

REVIEW

1. b   3. a   5. c

2. a   4. b   6. b

PRACTICE

A. What is your day like? *(More than one answer is possible. Check with your instructor or tutor.)*

__ Take my dog for a walk. _____

_____

_____

_____

_____

_____

_____

_____

_____

_____

_____

B. What is most important? *(More than one answer is possible. Check with your instructor or tutor.)*

C. Whoops! Schedule change. *(More than one answer is possible. Check with your instructor or tutor.)*

I would not eat dinner with my family.

_____

_____

_____

_____

_____

D. Describe a free day. *(More than one answer is possible. Check with your instructor or tutor.)*

First, I would stay in bed until 10:00 a.m.

_____

_____

_____

_____

_____

REVIEW

1. c	3. b	5. b
2. c	4. a	6. c

PRACTICE

A. Filling out forms.

Judith Ann Henry is looking for a job as a hostess at a small restaurant in her neighborhood. She lives at 15 Stuart Avenue in Detroit, Michigan. The zip code is 48201. She has lived there for ten years. Judith was born on July 16, 1962 in Chicago, Illinois. Her home telephone number is (313) 555-5423. She does not have a job yet so she has no work phone. Her Social Security number is 111-67-9145. Judith has two children. Her children's names are Robert and Martin. Her husband died in 1988.

<table>
<tr><td colspan="6" align="center">PERSONAL DATA
(Please print)</td></tr>
<tr><td>Name</td><td colspan="2">Henry
(Last)</td><td colspan="2">Judith
(First)</td><td>Ann
(Middle)</td></tr>
<tr><td>Address</td><td colspan="5">15 Stuart Avenue
(No. & Street)</td></tr>
<tr><td></td><td colspan="2">Detroit,
(City)</td><td colspan="2">MI
(State)</td><td>48201
(Zip)</td></tr>
<tr><td colspan="3">Permanent address same as above
(No. & Street)</td><td colspan="3"></td></tr>
<tr><td colspan="2">(City)</td><td colspan="2">(State)</td><td colspan="2">(Zip)</td></tr>
<tr><td colspan="3">Home phone: (313) 555-5423
Work phone: —</td><td colspan="3">Social Security no.
111 – 67 – 9145</td></tr>
<tr><td colspan="2">Date of birth
  7 / 16 / 62</td><td colspan="2">Age
Answer will vary.</td><td colspan="2">Place of birth
Chicago, Illinois</td></tr>
<tr><td colspan="6">Marital status
☐ Single ☐ Married ☐ Divorced ☐ Separated ☒ Widowed</td></tr>
<tr><td colspan="2">Spouse's name Deceased
(Last)</td><td colspan="2">(First)</td><td colspan="2">(Middle)</td></tr>
<tr><td colspan="2">Spouse's date of birth
—</td><td colspan="2">Age
—</td><td colspan="2">Place of birth
—</td></tr>
<tr><td colspan="2">Other dependents

  2</td><td colspan="4">Dependents' names

Robert and Martin</td></tr>
</table>

B. What would you say?

1. Eddie is filling out a form to apply for a job. He has made a lot of mistakes. He crossed them out.

   __He should ask for a new form.__ _____

   _____

2. Luisa's husband died a short time ago. She is filling out a form at the bank. Luisa is not sure what *marital status* means. She does not know which box to mark.

   She should mark "widowed." _____

   _____

3. Suki works in a hotel kitchen. She is divorced and has three children. Her 70-year-old mother lives with them and is ill. Suki does not know what to write for *no. of dependents*.

   She should write "4." _____

   _____

4. Jill is renting a room while she looks for an apartment. She wants to get training to be a cook's assistant. The form she must fill out at a night school asks for a permanent address.

   She should write a relative's address. _____

   _____

5. Al has been married two years. He is filling out a form at the supermarket. He want to be able to cash checks there. What should he write on the line asking for *spouse's name*?

   He should write his wife's name. _____

   _____

REVIEW

1. b   3. b   5. a
2. a   4. b   6. a

PRACTICE

A. Where could they fit in? *(More than one answer is possible. Check with your instructor or tutor.)*

1. Joyce is good with numbers and is very friendly to people.

   She could be a cashier in a restaurant. Or she

   could be a waitress.

2. Simon is shy and artistic. He would like to use his artistic ability in a food-service job.

   Simon could arrange food in special designs on plates.

   He could bake bread in fancy shapes or decorate cakes.

3. Gena loves children. She would like to have a food-service job where she can be with children.

   Gena could work in a school cafeteria.

4. Louis grew up on a farm and loves to cook and bake at home.

   He could be a cook or cook's assistant in the kitchen

   of a restaurant. Or he could be a baker.

B. Is this the right job?

```
┌─────────────────────────────────────────┐
│             Assistant Cook               │
├─────────────────────────────────────────┤
│                                          │
│ Large restaurant needs assistant cook who│
│ can work well under pressure.  Responsible│
│ for preparing salads and vegetable dishes.│
│ Some weekend work required.  One–two     │
│ years' experience needed.  Come to 10    │
│ Main St. for an interview and ask for Rita or│
│ Charles.  No calls please.               │
│                                          │
└─────────────────────────────────────────┘
```

		YES	NO
1.	Is this a good job for someone who can handle pressure?	√	
2.	Would you probably need to cut vegetables for this job?	√	
3.	Should you apply for this job if you have no experience?		√
4.	Do they want people to call before coming in for an interview?		√
5.	Would a person who can work on weekends be right for this job?	√	
6.	Do you think you would do well in this job?		

GLOSSARY

This glossary provides definitions of the more difficult words used in this book. The glossary is in alphabetical order. The definition of each word tells how the word is used in this book. The numbers in parentheses tell where the word is used for the first time.

Abbreviation A shortened form of a word or words. We see and use abbreviations every day. An example of an abbreviation is *c.* for *cup*. (Unit 15)

Ability Skill; to be good at something. He had a lot of musical ability. He decided to become a singer. (Unit 20)

Accurately Exactly. He tried to measure everything very accurately. It took him longer, but the cake turned out well. (Unit 15)

Aisle A row in the grocery store. Eggs are in the first aisle. (Unit 4)

Ambulance a special van used to move people who are sick or hurt. The ambulance came quickly after the car accident. (Unit 14)

Appliance Things, such as a toaster or coffee maker, to use in the home. Appliances make it easier to cook. (Unit 10)

Avoid To stay away from. Avoid drinking coffee if it makes you nervous. (Unit 2)

Balanced The right amount of the foods we need to be healthy. A balanced diet has food from the main food groups. (Unit 1)

Bleach Cleaning supply used to make things white and clean. Margo used bleach to make her clothes white. (Unit 10)

Booklet A small book. The dentist gave her a booklet about taking care of her teeth. (Unit 9)

Brand The company that makes a product. What brand is that bread? The label says it is made by the Good Bread Company. (Unit 4)

Calorie The unit of energy in food. There are about three hundred calories in a cheese sandwich. (Unit 16)

Carbon monoxide CO, a highly dangerous poisonous gas. Too much carbon monoxide in a room can kill you. (Unit 13)

Career A job someone chooses and continues to do for a long time. She worked her whole life as a doctor. Her career lasted more than 50 years. (Unit 20)

Cavity A hole in a tooth. The dentist found a cavity in the boy's tooth. (Unit 9)

Circulation The movement of blood through the body. The elderly man felt cold because he had poor circulation. (Unit 17)

Column Vertical section of the page. His name was in the first column on the page. (Unit 1)

Container Something used to hold something else. Martha likes to put her food in plastic containers. (Unit 7)

Contamination Made dirty or impure by contact. It is easy to contaminate food if you do not wash your hands carefully. (Unit 6)

Coupon A small piece of paper a company prints. You can use a coupon to save money when you buy something. Maria used a 25-cent coupon for soap and a 50-cent coupon for bread. She saved 75 cents. (Unit 3)

Day-care center A place children stay during the day while their parents work. Bob's son went to the day-care center near Bob's job. (Unit 18)

Dental hygienist Someone trained to clean and care for your teeth. The dental hygienist showed me how to floss and brush properly. (Unit 9)

Dependent Person who is taken care of financially by someone else. He has two dependents, his son and his wife. (Unit 19)

Detective A person who tries very carefully to get information. The police detective tried to find out who broke the windows at the school. (Unit 4)

Detergent Soap used to wash dishes and clothes. She keeps her detergent under the sink. (Unit 10)

Determine To decide. How much we sleep helps determine how we feel. Most people feel tired if they do not sleep enough. (Unit 1)

Diet The food a person usually eats. His diet is mostly fish, rice, and vegetables. (Unit 1)

Disconnect To take the battery out or unplug so that something no longer works. Never disconnect a smoke detector. If you do, it cannot warn you that there is a fire. (Unit 11)

Discover To learn; to find out. Sarah discovered that her neighbor worked for the same company. Now they drive to work together. (Unit 18)

Dispatcher A person who sends the help you need. The 911 dispatcher called the police for the man and woman. (Unit 14)

Economical Practical; not too expensive. An economical meal does not cost a lot of money. (Unit 5)

Elderly Old (person). Elderly people can often ride the bus for less. (Unit 16)

Elevate To raise up. He elevated his hand to stop the bleeding. (Unit 12)

EMT Emergency medical technician; person trained to give emergency care, especially for heart attacks. The EMT in the ambulance elevated the man's head. (Unit 14)

Equivalent Equal; the same. Eight ounces and one cup are equivalent. (Unit 15)

Extension cord An electric cord used to make the cord on something longer. Never use an extension cord on a coffee maker. Someone can pull it and get hurt. (Unit 10)

Fire prevention Keeping fires from happening. Everyone has to think about fire prevention. What can we do to keep fires from starting? (Unit 11)

First aid Emergency help for someone who is hurt or sick. When he cut his leg, I gave first aid until we got to the hospital. (Unit 12)

Floss A thin thread used to clean teeth; to use floss to clean one's teeth. Martin bought some floss at the drugstore. He flosses his teeth every night. (Unit 9)

Food scraps Pieces of food that will not be eaten. Sarah put the food scraps in the trash. (Unit 6)

Frustration Feelings of anger. He could not fix his car. He went for a walk to help get rid of his frustration. (Unit 17)

Germ A small living thing that can make you sick. There are germs on chicken, so wash it before you cook it. (Unit 6)

Habit Something we do regularly. He wakes up at six a.m. every day. Waking up early is his habit. (Unit 2)

Handle To touch; to work with. It is important to have clean hands when you handle food. (Unit 6)

Identify To know; to recognize. The teacher had a paper with no name on it. She could not identify whose it was. (Unit 5)

Impression The feeling someone has about someone else because of what the person said or did. Martin filled out a form for a job. His neat form made a good impression. He got the job. (Unit 19)

Impulse Suddenly; on an urge. Sally went to the store to get some milk. She saw some cookies and bought them on impulse. She had not planned to get them, but they looked so good. (Unit 3)

Increase To make more. He increased the number of hours that he sleeps at night. He used to sleep six hours, but now he sleeps eight hours. (Unit 17)

Ingredient Material a food product is made with. The ingredients in that cereal are oats, wheat, sugar, honey, and salt. (Unit 4)

Intake What we eat or drink. He eats about 4000 calories a day. His caloric intake is 4000 calories. (Unit 16)

Label The paper with writing on a bottle or box. It tells you about the product. Thomas read the label on the soup to see what it was made with. (Unit 3)

Leftovers Food from a meal you save to use later. On Wednesday we ate leftovers from Tuesday. (Unit 7)

Manage To organize. Mary has trouble managing her time. She is always late. (Unit 18)

Marital status Whether a person is married, single, divorced, separated, or widowed. Sue just changed her marital status. She got married last Saturday. (Unit 19)

Mechanical Having to do with machines or tools. The boy had a lot of mechanical ability. He loved to fix cars. (Unit 20)

Operator A person to call for help by dialing "0" on the telephone. The operator helped him call an ambulance. (Unit 14)

164

Overnight For the whole night; from night to the next morning. The cat stayed outdoors overnight. She was cold in the morning. (Unit 7)

Paramedic Person, other than a doctor, trained to do medical work. Four paramedics helped at the big fire downtown. (Unit 14)

Physical Using your body. Running and swimming are good physical exercise. (Unit 16)

Pilot light A small jet of gas that should always burn on a stove. I smelled gas when I got home. The pilot light on my stove had gone out. I lit it again. (Unit 13)

Plaque A material that forms on the teeth. Plaque is bad for your gums. Flossing your teeth helps get rid of plaque. (Unit 9)

Preparation (area) Counter or table in a kitchen where food is prepared for cooking. The preparation area should always be kept clean. (Unit 6)

Pressure Pushing against something. Pressure on the cut helped stop the bleeding (Unit 12)

Product Something sold at a store. That store sold many products such as food, tools, and furniture. (Unit 3)

Recognize To know; to be familiar with. I recognized my brother's voice when I picked up the telephone. (Unit 13)

Refrigerate To keep in the refrigerator. Harold refrigerates peanut butter to keep it fresh. (Unit 7)

Require To say something must be done. My job requires that I get there at seven a.m. I must be there on time. (Unit 4)

Requirement What we need. You have to be 18 years old and live in the state to vote. Those are the requirements. (Unit 16)

Rinse To pour water over something to take away what is on it. He rinsed the soap from the dishes. (Unit 6)

Rush To hurry. The two men rushed to catch the train. They had to run fast to get there in time. (Unit 18)

Salve A thick cream used on the skin as medicine. The cool salve made the boy's sunburn feel better. (Unit 12)

Section The area in a store where something is sold. Robert went to the dairy section to get some milk and butter. (Unit 5)

Serving The amount of food or drink we eat at one time. One cup of milk is a serving of milk. (Unit 1)

Smoke detector A machine that warns you if something is burning. Every home should have at least one smoke detector. (Unit 11)

Social Security number Nine-digit number needed to work in the United States. He had to get a Social Security number before he could get a job. (Unit 19)

Solve To find an answer to something. We could not solve the problem with the car. It just would not go. (Unit 17)

Spark A tiny flash of electricity. A small spark can start a big fire. (Unit 13)

Specials Products on sale at a store. Specials usually cost less than the regular price. (Unit 3)

Spill To make something fall or flow out by accident. Martin knocked over his glass. He spilled milk all over the floor. (Unit 6)

Spoil To become rotten and not safe to eat. Arnie left some meat out overnight and it spoiled. He could not eat it. (Unit 7)

Spouse One's husband or wife. Bob's spouse is two years younger than he is. He is 32, and his wife is 30. (Unit 19)

Spray To go out into the air. He shook the bottle before he opened it, so the soda sprayed all over the room. (Unit 8)

Spread To cause other people to get a disease. A cold can spread quickly in a school. (Unit 8)

Standard The same everywhere. Two cups that are standard hold the exact same amount. (Unit 15)

Sterilize To make something completely clean and free of germs. He sterilized the needle before he used it. The needle had no germs on it. (Unit 12)

Store To put away to use later. It is good to store food in tight containers. (Unit 7)

Store brand The label from the store. At the Big G Grocery, the store brand is Fun Foods. Many foods such as bread, vegetables, and milk have the Fun Foods label. (Unit 5)

Stressed Nervous; tense. Working all day in a hot, noisy room made Mark stressed. (Unit 17)

Suit To be right (for someone). He did not enjoy working with people. He was not suited to be a teacher. (Unit 20)

Support To provide someone with money and things needed to live. Martha supported her children and husband after he got hurt at work. (Unit 19)

Synthetic Man-made material; for example, polyester. His shirt burned quickly because it was synthetic. (Unit 11)

Unattended Not watched. Miriam left the baby unattended only a few minutes. The baby pulled the tablecloth. Dishes and hot coffee fell on the baby. (Unit 10)

Unit of measurement A carefully measured amount used by everyone to measure. *Inch* and *mile* are units of measurement we use often. (Unit 15)

Utensils Tools used for cooking and eating. Knives and spoons are common utensils. (Unit 6)

Utility Utilities are public services such as water and electricity. The utility companies in my hometown are very good. (Unit 13)

Ventilation A way to let fresh air in and old air out. Danny opened the window for better ventilation. (Unit 11)

Virus A type of germ that can make us sick. A cold is caused by a virus. (Unit 8)

Waitperson Waiter or waitress who serves food in a restaurant. The waitpersons at the restaurant were all very nice and helpful. (Unit 20)